BEING CH

The formation of Christian community

ROBIN GREENWOOD

First published in Great Britain in 2013

Society for Promoting Christian Knowledge
36 Causton Street
London SW1P 4ST
www.spckpublishing.co.uk

The author and publisher have made every effort to ensure that the
external website and email addresses included in this book are correct
and up to date at the time of going to press.
The author and publisher are not responsible for the content,
quality or continuing accessibility of the sites.

British Library Cataloguing-in-Publication Data
A catalogue record for this book is available from the British Library

ISBN 978-0-281-06935-4
eBook ISBN 978-0-281-06936-1

Typeset by Caroline Waldron, Wirral, Cheshire
First printed in Great Britain by Ashford Colour Press
Subsequently digitally printed in Great Britain

eBook by Graphicraft Ltd, Hong Kong

Produced on paper from sustainable forests

To all who are seeking to be Church for the world's repairing

'The message of this book will offer encouragement to many who hope for a Church that is increasingly collaborative, and one where clergy and laity can operate with mutual respect. Robin Greenwood's familiar forward-looking voice discusses theological and practical issues, exploring possibilities and suggesting alternative approaches. He advocates distinctive roles for priests and for other laity, pointing towards some ways in which expectations of clergy contributions might be re-envisaged, and interdependent relationships developed. Those who want the term "the Body of Christ" to become more than an oft-repeated phrase will find the book raises numerous core questions and ideas for reflection!'
Joanna Cox, National Adviser in Adult Education and Lay Development

'Robin Greenwood draws on an immense amount of practical experience in this short book. He writes with theologically informed realism about the life of the local church. There is much here to encourage and hearten all who care about the future of parish ministry.'
Nicholas Sagovsky, Whitelands Professorial Fellow, Roehampton University

'For some time now I have thought that "virtue ecclesiology" might have something important to offer to the Church in its continual task of re-inventing itself. In this book, Robin Greenwood provides a demanding and thought-provoking theory–practice synthesis, drawing particularly on the work of the moral philosopher Alasdair MacIntyre. The creative identification of the core practices of the local church, the virtues that are required to support these practices, and the importance of institutionalizing these practices both locally and in the wider Church in a way that is both faithful and life-giving, provides a novel way of thinking about Church as organization. There is much here that will help with down-to-earth practicalities, but set within a framework that will reward sustained reflection.'
Geoff Moore, Professor of Business Ethics,
Durham University Business School, and Reader in the Church of England

'When a thoughtful and considered tome is written regarding the reasons for and challenges to "being Church", it warrants our attention. In Robin Greenwood's *Being Church*, the question "Where to from here?" is asked. And the responses have far less to do with structures and strategies than they do with living in and through our eucharistic relationships. In my experience and estimation, our relationships and the ways in which "we are together" inform and give shape to our own responses to one another. It is my pleasure to commend this book to you as I believe, using the language of *A New Zealand Prayer Book, He Karakia Mihinare o Aotearoa*, that its words will encourage us "to hear what the Spirit is saying to the Church".'
The Rt Revd David Rice, Bishop of Waiapu,
Anglican Church in Aotearoa, New Zealand and Polynesia

'There are rich learnings here on how the whole body of Christ can be imbued with the values of the kingdom. The movement is from strategies to living out gospel virtues. *Being Church* is brimming with examples of how the people of God can exercise their baptismal calling in full partnership with the ordained. Personally, I was nourished and encouraged by visions and worked examples of lay people growing in discipleship. My own fifteen years' positive experience of team ministry has been challenged and stretched. As mixed economy and emerging forms of church beg new questions, this book grasps nettles of how "church" is to be worked out, both at the deep level of values or virtues, and at the everyday level of how ministry is shared.'

The Revd Canon Alastair Macnaughton, Director of Developing Discipleship,
Lindisfarne Regional Training Partnership

'Robin Greenwood's *Being Church* expands our vision of what we as God's people are called to be and do. This inspiring and insightful integration of theology and practical approaches to ministry speaks to those of us who seek new ways to renew Christian community. This work draws on insights from a variety of disciplines. It bases ministry in the theology of the Trinity and encourages the reader to engage in ministry in a relational and collaborative manner. Diocesan leaders are invited to move from inherited patterns of hierarchy that foster dependency, to a relational way of being Church within the complex reality of the twenty-first century. While acknowledging the tension between the priesthood of all believers and the ordained priesthood, this book offers a fresh perspective that calls us to a new relational and mutually respectful way of working together as the whole people of God. This is a great book to share with my colleagues in ministry development!'

The Revd Canon Sandra Holmberg, Missioner for Total and Shared Ministry,
The Episcopal Church, Minnesota, USA

'Robin Greenwood has long written and reflected on the re-imagining of priesthood in the contemporary Church. This book draws on his recent experience of returning to be a parish priest again, and combines his theological wisdom with a deep reflection on parish ministry. As always, there is delicacy, insight and theological depth, which speaks powerfully to the sense of powerlessness felt by many Christians. The sense of trying to keep alive a vision of hope, while immersed in the struggle to create a Church that embodies Christian wisdom, makes the book very relevant to many clergy.'

The Revd Canon Peter Sedgwick, Principal, St Michael's College, Cardiff

Contents

About the author

Robin Greenwood is a practical theologian with over forty years' experience as an Anglican priest, educator and writer. He is a member of the Third Order of St Francis and a visiting fellow at St John's College, Durham. He is married to Claire, also an Anglican priest. They have two sons and a daughter and four grandchildren.

Acknowledgements

This book could never have been written without the varied and highly gifted team of clergy, Readers and laity I have had the privilege to lead for over seven years in the parish of St Mary the Virgin, Monkseaton. I am grateful for their willingness to risk seeking a church that is participative and life-giving and generously to allow me time to reflect, write and connect with churches elsewhere.

I wish to extend a huge thank-you to a host of people for their contributions to the imagining and crafting of this book. Recent opportunities to contribute to consultations have been important: the Church of England Adult Education Network, the North East Practical Theology Intentional Conversation Group, the Liverpool Diocese Rural Group, the Rural Theology Association, the Newcastle Diocese Larger Churches Group and the Diocese of Lincoln. Membership of the Board and Development Group of the Lindisfarne Regional Training Partnership and the Strategic Development Group of the Diocese of Newcastle has also contributed to my understanding of the dynamics of contemporary church life and shaping of formational programmes for clergy and Readers.

For conversations at various depths on the theology–practice of church today I want to express thanks especially to Alan Bartlett, Katy Bell, David Bryan, Mike Burson-Thomas, Benjamin Carter, Val Cowan, Fraser Charlton, Joanna Cox, Richard Crossland, Jenny Dawson, Nicola Denyer, David F. Ford, Thelma Gilhespy, Tim Greenwood, Malcolm Grundy, Jane Hanson, Sue Hart, David Hewlett, Richard Hill, Carole and David Lax, Barrie Lawless, Tom McGuinness, John McDermott, Alastair Macnaughton, Pat Moran, Alison and Geoff Moore, Eileen Noble, Stephen Pickard, Jo and Neill Porter, Jenny Rowling, Nicholas Sagovsky, Kate Stobart and Richard Thornton. So many of the insights in this book have arisen through sharing in reflection with my wife, Claire, on the pains and joys of birthing mature and loving forms of Church.

Parish administrators Ruth Blake and Dot Clarke have contributed to the practical possibility for me to have time for reflection and writing. I continue to be grateful for the encouragement and skill of the SPCK editing team and especially to Ruth McCurry.

Introduction

In a lost world looking for maps, churches fired by the gospel have a vital role. Confident not in ideals and clarity but in the trustworthiness of relationships formed by God's love, churches can become honest, open, infectious and challenging communities for the sake of humanity and Creation. My purpose here is to encourage Christian communities to revisit their ways of being Church and be present to what emerges through the voice of the Holy Spirit and of society.

The paradox at the heart of the Church's life at present has made this book particularly difficult to write. In the 50th anniversary year of Vatican II, despite the great surge of hope generated by the Council being tempered by many negative experiences of Church, sparks of the fire of the Holy Spirit are still flying. Three kinds of Church especially appear to be flourishing: those that adopt a single vision with a strong articulate leadership, cathedrals offering a glimpse of the numinous, and Pentecostal churches. As we shall explore, hope and despair now go hand in hand in the lives of local churches, lay and ordained ministers, and dioceses or regions of the Church.

On the one hand, dioceses, churches and clergy increasingly speak of mission and evangelism; there is a growing acceptance of the partial truths of all the churches; the number and degree of responsibility of women in public ministries increase; liturgical imagination expands; fresh expressions of Church are now in the bloodstream; mixed-mode ways of being Church continue to be explored; church justice and peace groups display energy; and all God's people are cooperating as never before.

And yet, on the other hand, many churches are low in numbers and energy; many of the stipendiary clergy who have worked stoically for decades are retiring and their successors are working differently; there are increasingly unrealistic expectations of clergy as inherited patterns become unsustainable; multiple-parish arrangements are often causing severe stress to communities and to individuals; raising finance from aging congregations is an increasing source of anxiety; buildings are often a burden; many younger Christians have minimal interest in the historic and inherited structures; churches are tempted to retrench and focus on internal rather than local partnerships and kingdom agendas; dioceses stand in urgent need of a new understanding and practice of mission and yet find it extremely difficult to align sufficient energy, resource or volition.

These 13 short chapters present an urgent and sustained questioning of a church culture that evolved in a different world. Chapter 1 presents an operational theology rooted in the desire to live in the deeply patterned order Christians know as Trinitarian relatedness: an intensity of connection with God and Creation. Some who are suspicious of 'mere theory' will prefer to skip this or come back to it later. However, I do invite the reader to recognize the power of ideas interwoven with practice. It has been prayerful and networked wrestling with these theory–practices that has kept me resilient in living for so many decades on the inside of the outside of the Church.

A barrier to some will be my emphasis on the centrality of the Eucharist to Christian practice. Choosing to stand within a liberal Anglican tradition and encouraging a wide variety of liturgical patterns, I cannot imagine a Christian community life not focused on eucharistic celebration. For me this draws together Church as a baptized and baptizing community, as under Scripture and seeking to build goodness into society. From the earliest days of discipleship, Christian communities breaking bread together were formed through the Eucharist, a distillation of the whole of what they had received from Christ. Rather than looking for an impossible settlement that might accommodate everyone, we can choose to receive and celebrate the partial insights of all. Actively celebrating unity in difference is the fiery core of communal Christian belief and living. Some will also point out pragmatically that, with fewer clergy, sustaining a eucharistic focus will be unworkable. If we think we haven't sufficient priestly ministry we're looking in the wrong place.

For the sake of the contemporary world and in response to the leading of the Holy Spirit, for four decades I have dedicated my energy and skills to persuading the Church to re-invent itself. Increasingly I recognize that it is only in the present moment and place, and not in some great future plan, that new meaning, strength and peace are found. My present experience as parish priest has taught me to be less hopeful and less anxious about the future. Our calling is to respond to God at work within and through Christian community, formed through the overlapping of activity and stillness.

The Parable of the Sower (Matthew 13.1–23) illustrates the constant call for churches to be propagating seed with abandon, without controlling where it may lead. Matthew knew already how Christian communities emerge from the interweaving of love, despair, delight, failure, rejection, forgiveness, boredom and unexpected bursts of growth. This old yet new corporate Christian pathway binds us together through reason, emotion and faith in transformative practices that enshrine as much of God's desire as we can absorb today.

As I write, sea ice in the Arctic is shrinking to its smallest extent ever recorded (Vidal 2012). It remains to be seen whether we will shrug our shoulders and look forward to greater investment in drilling for more fossil fuels that will exacerbate the global situation. Or will it be a wake-up call to radically different approaches to energy creation? This is a parable for the churches. In this era of 'neo-atheism' and the individual's right to self-expression, to be nominally or passionately religious is equated with a naive loss of rationality or autonomy. The search in this volume is for a re-integrative approach to finding creative theory–practice for becoming Church for our society now.

1

Finding how to be Church again

Key virtues of a God-centred Christian community

We cannot be good shepherds and teachers
unless we are reborn in the Spirit
and allow ourselves to be led by God,
open to the new ways of God and truly open to people.
This means that we are dying to our own ego
and our need to be in control,
but also to our need to rebel and prove ourselves.

(Jean Vanier 2004, p. 80)

Centred on God

Our society is in many ways lost and anxiously searching for where we are on the map. Largely bemused as it is by religious commitment and cynical about faith in a loving God, there are signs of a restless seeking for ways of finding meaning and consolation. In baptism parties, bringing ever more people dressed in their most elegant clothes, we can see their longing for Church to have the pearl of great price, clues to the mystery at the heart of life. In the tragic funeral of a baby, churches humbly stand beside those who are numb with grief or full of anger, offering a uniquely safe space for grief and love. With a mixture of urgency and joy, Christian communities now have a particular opportunity to show hospitality to all who seek God. Christian communities need to remember that we have all the gifts we need to be Church, when we are open to God, to the world, to one another and to ourselves.

Being Church again, now, in the specifics of this place and time, requires a confident, and always searching, presumption of God's existence and of God being of a particular character. Making room for God to be God, and to love God only for God's sake, is central to this exploration. As Paul writes (Romans 8.26), it is the Holy Spirit

1

praying in us, calling us to the Father, that gives us Christian identity over anything we might do or pray. Knowing God, as truly as we can, guides and corrects our practice of Christian community.

God's nature

The Holy Spirit draws us to know God in the tender intimacy of sons and daughters, painfully refusing to endorse our prejudices or condone our own short-sighted desires.

'A ceaseless outgoing and return of the desiring God' (Coakley 2012, p. 4), is incompatible with a distant patriarchal monologue. To find how to be Church again, in our present context, needs our own hearts to be open to the intensity of God's love. Coakley continues, 'It is the Holy Spirit who "interrupts" my human monologue to a (supposedly monadic) God; it is the Holy Spirit who finally thereby causes me to see God no longer as a patriarchal threat but as infinite tenderness'. Worshipping and living out the mystery of the Trinity moves us beyond merely personal choice. It takes us towards the reciprocally ordered practice of Christian community and a serious but joyful sharing in the search for the flourishing of all people and Creation.

When, in the Eucharist, we say, 'In union with Christ, in the power of the Holy Spirit, we pray to the Father', we are describing the transfiguring life of Christian community.

Recovering relational ways of being Church will include at least some of the following elements.

Awareness of ourselves in our present circumstances

Moving beyond abstract theory, being Church demands that we make ourselves as fully present as we dare at this time. Engaging with and praying through this book, alone or with others, and holding in mind the local neighbourhood and churches, readers could ask:

- What are the realities of life here for very different sets of people?
- What difference is the Church making to people's lives in this area?
- What is of value in what I (and my church) do already and what could I change in line with God's purpose?
- In what ways is the Church more of a problem than a resource?
- Where is God's presence apparent here?

- Where could we join more in God's work?
- What can I personally contribute to a renewed Church?
- How can I be an encourager of those who are younger?
- How can I relieve the Church's anxiety by being more generous financially?
- Where can I help to create conversations that build up hope?
- How will I work or pray for God's Church to become more open and attractive to those who are hungry for hope?
- If I am an innovator already, how can I interweave what I have learnt with others in ways that are mutual and loving?
- How can I work with the people of the third age – the recently retired?
- How can I use people's natural interests to bring them closer to God?
- How can I and my church be more visible and courteously active in the wider neighbourhood?

Church lived in its practices

Gospel practices are social and cooperative, not activities carried out in isolation.

> Surely that is why bride and bridegroom, invitations to banquets, and wedding celebrations are Jesus' most common metaphors for eternal life. They imply reciprocity, the give and take of mutual reverence and mutual desire, and most of all, happiness.
> (Richard Rohr in Finley *et al.*, 2012)

Unlearning notions of Church as individuals who happen to turn up to services and social events requires a new common awareness, reached through preaching and living together the baptismal calling to be 'in Christ'. To be Church is to be ordered together as companions in faith, tears and joy. In a Church struggling to be 'grown up', from within our varied journeys we must love and tease one another into practices of vulnerability and interdependence. Heroically or lazily to soldier on being Church 'as we've always known it here' is in reality to cut ourselves off from 'Church'. Being Church is to be united within the group of all groups held by Christ and moving at the Spirit's direction in a mutually accountable relationality.

Practices of faith have been passed on from earlier generations, recapitulating time after time in ever new situations, following the way of Jesus since Pentecost. Churches are those who allow ourselves to be drawn towards God's final purposes now, in this moment. How we make ourselves present as Church in this situation tells the story of what we have absorbed of God's desire for the fulfilment of the world and its peoples.

Church for the formation of desire

As Church we are easily tempted to become distracted from our true identity and purpose. We are perhaps harassed by falling numbers, rising damp or too many parishes grouped together and diminishing clergy numbers. We may be disapproving and unforgiving of the behaviour of others. We will surely have disputes among musicians, fight over which version of Scripture to read, or scapegoat those whom we find difficult.

Taking into account the wisdom literature in Scripture and Jesus' own ease with touching, sensuality, tiredness, hunger, grief, anger, celebration, feasting, respect and compassion, we can recover, in our present contexts, Church rooted in God's intensity of love and movement towards us.

The invitation of Scripture is to let God be our primary obsession. Moses' decision to liberate his oppressed people was transformed from the moment when his attention was arrested at the bush that, burning, was not consumed (Exodus 3). He responded in awe; he removed his shoes in worship. God invites us now to stop and turn around, accepting the gift of illumination, our hearts burning and our purposes ventilated by the Holy Spirit. As God communicated to Moses a biased compassion for those in need of liberation, our society needs Church to hear this message and act on it now.

This 'towardness' that Scripture reveals is a reminder of how we are regarded by God and allured into participating in God's own ways with the world. Living in the Spirit, churches recover confidence that in all the mess of human interrelating, the central truth is that we are desired by God. As we become so assured, we grow in the self-esteem that allows us to participate in God's own desires. We also grow in confidence to let go of old securities and transcend our previous certainties.

4

Rowan Williams speaks of this movement in terms of going beyond what we used to hold as 'theologically correct' and so discerning a development in our belief. He describes this as a centring on the cross of Christ so that it may in turn permeate our ways of exercising and receiving authority. This movement is 'a steady and endless enlarging of the heart through union in prayer and virtue with the Word, which is also a steady and endless growth in knowledge of the Father' (Ford 2007, p. 220).

The interplay between desiring and receiving God's promises for the work of God's people is a core theme in the book of Revelation. Churches are invited to enter into God's knowledge, judgement, instructions, guidance, encouragement and promises. In learning what it is that God offers, churches are encouraged to receive these blessings as the most direct way of discovering their transformed identity. Their ultimate calling is for their names to be linked with the name of Jesus himself (Revelation 3.11–12). Directed by the Spirit, embraced by the Father, with all nations, in intimacy with Jesus in a meal-centred community, such churches can reveal to the world their most profound potential for the world's healing.

Called to unity, holiness, catholicity and apostolicity

Every genuine practice of Church is connected to every other. In the accumulated experience of the Church this is to become united, learn holiness, choose catholic order and learn to be apostolic. Whether in a cathedral or in 25 parishes held in plurality, being Church is Christian community that has certain characteristics:

- Being Church is being *united* as God's people (Psalm 133.1–3), celebrating difference, held up in prayer and learning God's many-layered wisdom and ministering from the Spirit's gifts (Ephesians 3.10). Such a church will offer hospitality, living out of God's abundant generosity, welcoming everyone, of any age, at all times and growing as God's people, for ever linked with the name of Jesus Christ (Ephesians 1.17–18 and 4.1–6).
- Being Church is desiring and learning *holiness* (Isaiah 6.3; Revelation 4.8). To desire holiness is to respond to the call of God to the people of God to be like God (1 Peter 1.14–16) in goodness and beauty (Psalm 19.7–10). The priority will be the transformation of

desire through prayer and worship: 'Come, Holy Spirit!' A church that is a school for holiness will be one where its people have chosen to let themselves be drawn towards God, rather than alternative distractions, and to praise in participation through kinds of music, words and action, celebrating with all who have gone before and those yet to come.

- Being Church is being in *catholic* interconnection with all Christians, Jews and all faiths open to being part of God's ways with the world (Ephesians 1.10; Genesis 12.3). The Church is its people dispersed and engaged in every aspect of human life and endeavour. This Church will flourish through engaging across boundaries and learning and contributing to learning to build up capacity and hope in neighbourhoods. Such a Church will be always looking out as well as building a house for creativity, sharing God through music, drama, literature, art, economics and politics. It will be keen to connect with people everywhere, sharing joy, pain and the search for sustainable futures (Genesis 12.1; Luke 9.23).

- Being Church is being a company of learners, teachers and sent ones (Matthew 28.16–20). Apostolicity is the gift and calling that combines the exercise of authority with obedience, worship, sending and being sent, being confidently identified with God who is Father, Son and Holy Spirit, passing on faith, welcoming stran-gers and showing how to be in communion with Jesus (Matthew 25.35, 40). Apostolicity begins in the sending by the Father of the Son and the Spirit so that in the world the Church can do what Jesus did in the power of the Spirit: healing the sick, feeding the hungry, drawing people back into relationship with God, and reconciling people and communities. It often means walking towards controversy and complex deliberation for the re-interpretation of faith in ever new situations. Such a Church will offer different paths of learning that help people pursue greater dignity in their everyday lives; it will be searching for new truth, with God at work in the everyday, and will be engaged in living faithfully, whatever life sends.

Searched and sustained by the Holy Spirit

Church identity, drawn from a wisdom interpretation of Christian tradition, explodes out of the worship of God and a discernment of God's true nature. Within the early centuries of Christianity, through worship, prayer and vigorous unfinished disputes, among Christian communities there has evolved the distinctive doctrine of God as Trinity.

Worship, as the core activity of Church, is the most potent aspect of being together in Christ. Through the structuring of practices and relationships, inward and outward, the Church's character is identified. Being Church is a constant exchange between inherited tradition and innovation. Tradition is the living reality of the Risen Christ in the Church and world today, made real through the Holy Spirit. Church is the embodied movement of the Spirit, creating simultaneously a stable and unpredictable environment. It is like an incredibly multi-coloured and variable-patterned piece of knitting that's still being worked on the needles. Within this transformational tradition-process, the work of the Holy Spirit periodically fosters the emergence of the prophetically new, which can be accepted as authentic when it is reformulated in discernible continuity with what Christians have previously recognized as God's transformative work (Luke 7.11–30).

So for churches serving the kingdom in the way of Jesus and led by the continuing work of the Holy Spirit, stability and change and continuity and the radically new are both embraced. Examples of this today are the constant renewal of the shape of the liturgy within an obvious continuity, the emergence of new expectations of the relation between those ordained and the Church as a whole through constant wrestling with Scripture and contemporary culture, and similarly, radically new expectations for women in ordained office.

The interrogation at the heart of the book of Job is, 'Can you honestly claim that you fear God for nothing?' (Job 1.9–12). In the wisdom tradition represented by Job, Jesus refuses to identify faith in God with the repetition of old truths in new situations. There is a decisive sign of the novelty of Jesus confirmed in the account of his baptism and temptations (Mark 1.9–12). The Holy Spirit, believed by fellow Jews to have been quenched since the last biblical prophet, comes to Jesus, who is in intimate relationship with the Father and called to reveal God's purpose. This is newness as fulfilment, not discontinuity, evident in his relationship with John the Baptizer who couldn't believe this was the One who was sent (Luke 7.19).

Central to Christian wisdom is Jesus' recalling of the Jewish truth that God is to be loved for God's sake. Jesus' prayer emphasizes the 'hallowing' or blessing of the name of God: loving God for God's sake, simply because God is God. His constant life and prayer is to serve God because God is God, practising obedience to God's will, even to laying down his life, as the end and purpose of Creation (Luke 11.1–4; 22.42; John 19.30). The great value of a wisdom approach to being Church is to see how the long Jewish–Christian tradition of learning in the school of the Holy Spirit invites us:

- to be wary of merely repeating past practices in new circumstances;
- to celebrate poetry, image and metaphor for conveying truth and growing imaginative vision;
- to notice how Scripture is itself a movement of tradition, containing new learning and breaks with past wisdom;
- to remain open to creative dispute about complex matters;
- to be alert to the immediate pains and joys of people;
- to pay particular attention to the voice of those who suffer or who have come through times of great difficulty;
- to sustain practices of kindness and care;
- to be deliberately open to God's searching and probing;
- to both receive and respond to God's love, call, questioning, possibilities, desire and purposes; and
- to be loved by God and to love God for God's sake.

Ordered in love

To speak of being 'ordered' gives us a jolt in today's society. Resisting patriarchal ways of thinking, we can re-imagine ordering as a way of following Jesus' invitation to give up our life to find it, not to expect to sit in the important chairs, and to redefine close relatives as those who do the will of the Father. As Paul insists, we are not only parts of Christ's body; we simply cannot be Church without one another.

Beyond planning and ideals, to dare to be ordered together means letting go of our preference. For churches used to functioning through manipulation or to handing over power to the most vociferous or long-established members, this is vertiginous learning. Parishes that formerly enjoyed proud independence are challenged to pool their resources and enjoy learning to enjoy one another.

It is an especial test of the integrity of bishops and priests to consider being 'ordered together' instead of assuming a right to shape churches according to our own predilections. To cultivate mature Church requires in each of us a journey towards self-awareness and a conscious willingness to be part of the corporate ordering. This radical gospel expectation demands that we allow God to address us (often through the friendship of others). Here we can find healing and authentic selfhood in accepting our wounds and taking support to grow through them.

In *Parish Priests* (Greenwood 2009) I drew out the possibilities for a corporate notion of the role of bishop (*episkope*, overseeing or watching out for) as an aspect of Church to which all can contribute, as opportunity arises. All organizations need to make judgements between greater and lesser degrees of complexity and on who has the expertise to benefit a given situation. It is also important that those with the capacity for seeing the whole picture are permitted to influence the Church's character and direction.

This is not about degrees of personal inner status. In a church setting out to echo Trinitarian relatedness, being ordered together is a willingness to recognize that on our own we are incomplete. Our true selves are formed in mutuality and church is a primary place to practise mutual service and friendship in love. It is vital that the present crises around clergy numbers that are forcing churches into networks can become a creative way of recovering the true identity of Church as interconnected rather than isolationist. This is a narrow and vital window of opportunity that we could easily miss. Communities of the entire people of God are those who willingly surrender themselves, as baptized into Christ and into one another, and who accept the invitation to live in mutual order, as one of another (Romans 12.5).

A navigating *episkope* shared by leaders, lay and ordained

There's someone with a spade in a garden. What is he or she doing? There are myriad possible and overlapping answers: digging over the soil, preparing the ground for planting, taking exercise, getting rid of the weeds that annoy the neighbours or seeking buried treasure. So when I put anything into my diary, chair a meeting or stand at the altar as priest, what am I doing? What are the guiding metaphors that might frame the work of those called in various ways to animate God's people? One of them, I believe, is *episkope*, watching out, together, for the people and work of the Church.

All baptized Christians, lay and ordained, are part of the lattices that constitute our life as Church. Priests and licensed ministers who share in *episkope* within the ministries and discipleships of a local church make particular contributions from their perception of the roles they occupy. The powerful reality is that just by being who we are and where we are, we set a tone. How vital it is that we do this in full awareness. It helps some to think of two lists – one written by the local priest and parishioners that asks, 'What is it, in different situations, that only I can do?' and another written by the wider Church, against which I can enquire, 'What is it that *the Church* is asking of *me in particular*, in *this ordained or licensed role*, in *this* set of circumstances?' How those lists match up or not is a matter for daily discernment, especially as priestly responsibilities are changing towards forms that are unpredictable, even five or ten years from now.

Presiding within the mission of a local Christian community is a role with a set of tasks that evolve in ever new circumstances. The capacity to exercise a presiding, watchful ministry is therefore vital. Even if we cannot name it, we can recognize it when we feel it in ourselves or see it in others. It can't be spelled out in terms of clever technique or even having a particular model or metaphor. *Top Gear* presenter James May, on the radio discussing his favourite music, said, first in relation to cars, 'It's not the amazing speed or the shiny technology that does it for me – it's beyond words, it's the *experience* – the "*drive*".' So with music, it's not the posh piano or the skill of the pianist that makes the difference, but the *musicianship*, working from one's deepest source.

In the rapidly changing flux of society now, what are we asking of priests and especially of those presiding among expanding teams of various kinds? This is a recurring question in what follows. For now, I would say that the equivalent of *musicianship* in priests is the connective spark that is the consequence of working from our deepest, God-focused, source. We need loving, resilient and wise priests who can live on the edge of the unexpected, handling attachment and detachment. We do not need heroic, autonomous, solo performers.

Recent literature on this subject of the role of the ordained or licensed leader has brought up many guiding metaphors, including navigating, midwifing or bridge-building, to give expression to the facilitative and animating role of priesthood. In a relational theology–practice of Church it is exceptional for the priest to travel alone. Partnership is the route. This could be through monthly meetings with leaders of the musical life of the parish, the Mothers' Union, the baptism preparation group . . .

A pledging group of three laity set themselves the task of raising a huge sum of money for the refurbishment of their church building. They invited people to small home meetings to hear about the refurbishment of the building. Beyond bricks and mortar, basic to their presentation was conversation about God, God's purposes and how the redesigned building could help celebrate their combined insights. Their priest occasionally needed to show an intense support and encouragement, but not micro-management.

Presiding in a spirit of mutuality

Here is an example from my own experience as vicar of a parish described by a colleague as 'middle-class, middle-of-the-road and middle-managers'. For six years it was a demanding, enjoyable and stimulating task until, suddenly, after a serious accident resulting in multiple injuries, I was unavailable to lead the ministry team for five months. After those years of intentionally working to become ordered together with me presiding, in my absence the team voiced a clear sense that although they were certainly motivated about the direction in which the parish was moving, the vicar remained the lynch-pin. Not only was I the final back-stop, I was the means through which conversations happened, the one who made sure that ministers were ministered to, and the one who enabled the community to make decisions to which as many as possible could subscribe. The development of email conversations between many key leaders, for example, meant that on a day-to-day basis I and others could see the way conversations were going towards projects or decisions without feeling a compulsion to contribute.

My sudden absence and the challenge, at some point in the future, of a vacancy and change of incumbent, focused the team's conversations. They asked,

> What is it that Robin does? He is the main means and hub of communication; he holds people to account for what they have agreed to do within what the church as a whole has identified as

its mission action plan; he ensures we have regular staff conversations that are more than diary meetings; ultimately he makes difficult decisions; he does the invisible fixes; he meets regularly with office holders to keep everything connected. But this is held by Robin's intentional practice and experience. It could very easily unravel with too detailed management and a differently tempered vicar. How do we exercise authority, ordered together but without a vicar?

How do we work now?

The conversation continued by asking, 'Theologically, what is the "polity" or undergirding theology of how the parish serves God?' Ecclesiastical polity is the way the Church operates and is governed through ministerial structures that are always connected in relationship with other churches, in the diocese and beyond. It is rooted in ecclesiology, the theological self-understanding of the Church as community and institution. So the question was, 'How do the different groups relate to one another (vicar, staff, wardens, church council, local ministry development team and the core groups for worship, learning and so on)?' They were aware that the collaborative culture and way of working we were trying to achieve would be very vulnerable to any structural solution.

The insight came that a permanent key question in the community is 'Who can I love and who will love me?' Too often the answer to this question had simply been the vicar: given the situation of my absence, the medium-term prospect of a vacancy and the long-term desire for a grown-up church, what other solutions were possible?

How do we have conversations?

One of the key Anglican moves is to be always in conversation. This is illustrated in the formal interrogations at an ordination service (of the archdeacon, the candidates and the congregation) before the bishop lays hands on the candidates. None of us comes to the conversations of church life as a private citizen: we come in a 'role' defined by the infinite 'triangulations' of conversations that define who we are in that place. So a cat's cradle of interconnection of the whole people of God, bishop, bishop's officer, parish priest and licensed minister share in the *episkope* of a church mutually ordered, bringing experience from life in the Church and the world.

These conversations of prayer, critical friendship and commitment make it catholic and in our case, Anglican. These webs and 'triangulations' of conversation define our catholic order. From this particular dilemma in one parish arise vital questions for a Church aspiring to interanimative rather than top-down dynamics. How far are people aware of the way they are already engaged in these conversations? Do they know the 'role' they are in, and how this makes us relate 'one with another'? Do we allow people to have the confidence to speak from that role with authority and power? How do the personality traits and preferred ways of operating of individuals inhibit or release energy?

Can we find a way of honouring, marking and defining these conversations so that they show our discernment is intimately connected to the continuing life of the Church: the body of Christ, filled by the Holy Spirit for the sake of the kingdom, in which we are all intimately part, one with another?

The kingdom can't be brought in by our hard work

The conversation of the staff team finally considered the dis-ease between aspiring to be a church of all its people and the actual situation in which people are in danger of 'burn-out' through the Church's new expectations. What mutual care needed to be drawn out? The pressure of time meant that, like many churches, we were always at risk of being governing bodies of business and not following our primary task, which is discerning God's desires for what the Church should be doing here. The kingdom of grace, freedom and God's abundance, as demonstrated in the life of Jesus, cannot be brought in by the overworking or control of a minority.

So the questions arose, 'How could the community allow the Holy Spirit to be part of this, to give comfort to the disturbed, and to disturb the comfortable, to help us discern what God is calling us to do?' 'But how do we "discern" differently from the security of hearing the vicar's opinion?' 'How can we create safe places for discernment and honour the voices of those from our community who might tell us most clearly what the Holy Spirit is calling us to be?'

The desire was expressed for the staff team, groups making up the life of the church (church council, local ministry development team, wardens and the core groups) to base their lives more intensely on prayer, in whatever form that takes, to allow space for this discernment. 'If we are not, how can we be sure that we are building up the kingdom and not just "massaging" our sense of our own importance?' Undergirding all of this, an urgent need was discerned to generate a culture of reciprocity for sharing care, nurture and spiritual guidance, so that all engaged in the community might grow in faith and confidence as a sure sign of the kingdom among us.

It took my enforced absence for several months, meeting with individual staff members and wardens occasionally, for the practice of collegiality to grow more strongly. I hope that churches in many different circumstances could make connections with this narrative. How much more trusting in the Holy Spirit it would be for churches to imagine and choose to foster reciprocal ways of operating, without this requiring the stipendiary priest to be ill or absent.

As one priest told a conference recently when speaking of worship for those exploring faith, 'It can't rely on me, so others got involved.' She described how Messy Church started slowly as she walked with people until they started asking questions. Then, when she left that church, it fell apart but then started up again. The image of God she associated with that narrative was one of welcome and love – it was not so much a matter of arrival as a place of being with God.

A similar story came to me from a group of Lincolnshire parishes. In facilitating an all-age nativity play with a cast of almost 80, a Reader described exploring the fine balance between 'pushing things on' and believing enough in the commitment of the people involved to take risks. The joyful energy here came from the rigorous prayer life that was her bedrock.

Eucharistic celebration: measure of measures

The corporate practice of celebrating the Eucharist, in a multitude of ways, is a lens for recognizing relationality as the gospel shape of Church. As I have suggested in *Being God's People* (Greenwood and Hart 2011), my own Anglican practice of the Spirit-led celebration of the Eucharist, as ordered spontaneity and non-identical repetition, a recapitulation of Pentecost, is pivotal for building up the church to serve God's desire. In this present study I would regard it as the key practice that can hold together the local church's inner development with its impact on the neighbourhood and world.

What might it mean to become 'a walking church', generated by the gospel and restlessly finding ultimate purpose in Jesus' proclamation of the kingdom? This is not a fixed set of rules but a contingent way of living in relation to that final connection with God, humanity and Creation that is part of the human journey as well as its goal:

> Ongoing learning saves the aging from becoming more fossil-ized than transformed. The problem with aging is not age, it is petrification, rigidity of soul, inflexibility. Only ideas keep ideas flowing. When we close our minds to what is new, simply because we decide not to bother with it, we close our minds to our responsibility to ourselves – and to others – to keep on growing. (Chittister 2008 p. 98)

Eucharist is the practical activity that creates Church – in which Christians learn how to share in the life, death and resurrection of Jesus Christ. It is the pure primal event by which the world was recon-stituted in Jesus' time, and it is made present with each re-enactment. Eucharist measures the Church by measuring the quality of each member's journey to God within the company of any given church and in companionship with all churches and all Creation.

Daniel Hardy reflected that although Scripture measures the Church, it is the Eucharist that is the ultimate measure. The Church was breaking bread to remember Jesus long before it formulated what we call the New Testament. 'Measure' does not imply being judge-mental or a fixed ideal, because the measuring encompasses the cir-cumstances and effect of the measuring itself. Rather, the Eucharist measures by naming the element of church practice that most clearly typifies the whole: that is, acknowledging and celebrating God's redemptive presence in the life of the Church. Priests and others gather God's people to be formed as church through one another, through the shaping of the building, through Scripture, peace, bread and wine and being sent away. So through the Spirit our inner desires are re-formed; drawn towards God, we are extended together towards the world for its integration.

Reflecting on his own final illness, Hardy scaled over from medical to theological language the process of 'granulation'. This scientific term refers to the way wounds heal from connective tissue deep within the flesh. He was reflecting on how healing is intrinsic to ourselves, rather than merely done to us. The narrative of the woman who suffered from haemorrhages (Luke 8.40–48) makes a connection between Jesus' walking and healing with the transformation of the whole person and community through ordinary meetings and exchanges. The woman who suffered chronic bleeding touches Jesus' cloak. Luke makes the point that through the sheer power of Jesus' presence, this healing goes very deep. When communities gather for Eucharist we bring our deepest wounds, hoping that a profound shift will take place within and between us.

> Granulation . . . it reaches down that deep. That's the redemptive side: that filtering goes all the way down, far more down than people realize . . . Letting be in a very real sense, something springing up. Letting one's own fullness come out.
>
> (Hardy 2010, p. 118)

This notion of granulation as a knitting together of things in God's Spirit, beyond anything we can imagine, has clear links with the notion of 'presencing'. Communities and groups are healed at a deep level and can act in mutual adult dynamics when the Spirit is allowed to well up beyond formality and rationality. One image of a general medical practitioner today is of a 'mountain guide' to our whole selves as we take full responsibility for our health, as well as supporting and sometimes intervening so that we remain well or are assisted with our healing. Christ's presence in Scripture and Eucharist have infinite potential for healing, but from the inside, not the outside. The profound longed-for transformation arises from within communities and persons living in a *habitus* in which faith practices are embedded, where we are read by Scripture, measured by Eucharist and so regenerated by Jesus (see Proverbs 6.6; 30.24–25).

The nameless virtue

We shall also be resourced in this exploration by the revival in virtue ethics to explore how a 'virtue ecclesiology' could help the Church harmonize its own acting and being more ethically. For Aquinas the heart of the life of faith lies in receiving the gifts of the Holy Spirit.

Eleonore Stump suggests the analogy of enzymes to connect the gifts of the Spirit with theological virtues, especially that of love. After giving a scientific definition of the work of enzymes, she reflects:

> for Aquinas, the gifts of the Holy Spirit have the effect of anchoring the infused theological virtues [faith, hope and love] more deeply in a person's psyche and enabling them to have their desired effect there. The gifts of the Holy Spirit as-it-were cement the infused virtues into the psyche. (Stump 2012, p. 96)

A renewed emphasis on relationality helps us to recognize why analogical ways of discovery are preferable to their binary and adversarial alternatives. Such approaches to the practice of faith most truly bear witness to God who is Trinity, mysterious and present, transcendent and incarnate. So, for example, trans-local movements for change require us not to create oppositional or dual process models demanding either–or choice. We shall consider how this will enliven the relation between institution and local church, between clergy and laity, bishop and priest, or between one form of learning and another. The Jesuit Karl Rahner (1992, p. 34) proposed a 'nameless virtue' as essential for the life of Church, locally and universally. He spoke of the virtue of absolute respect for the mutual relationship of theory and practice, of knowledge and freedom, and at the same time respect for their dissonance. It is the virtue of the unity and diversity of realities without which one would be sacrificed in favour of the other. The nameless virtue celebrates the consciousness of intuition together with that of articulation. What is on offer is the development of a new way of understanding the world and of being human within it that is slowly taking collective shape.

An example of a parish learning to be ordered in mutual respect

I can perhaps illustrate the search for the nameless virtue from the painful yet releasing experience of the holding of a public hearing of the Consistory Court in our own church nave. As a seaside suburb with some of the lowest poverty indicators in the North East, we are on the whole very privileged. But a gospel invitation to be ordered together in love and purpose can be seen as highly subversive to an individualist culture. We find we are constantly vulnerable to distractions: when the older generation fails to trust the ones now in leadership or when people become fixated on a single issue rather than seeing the whole.

Over a ten-year period there was a discernment by the church council that not only did the church need to catch up on housekeeping (boiler, lighting, decoration) but a number of physical changes would tell us more of the intimacy and inclusiveness of the Trinity. It would also make the building better suited for contemporary worship and for wider use for drama, art exhibitions, concerts and neighbourhood events. The majority of people trusted the group appointed to lead change, listening carefully to presentations and examining exhibitions. Making public decisions about practical and aesthetic issues requires a general trust in one another as compromises have to be reached without losing the central vision.

Discerning when to end conversations and move forward requires courage and determination but brings its rewards. One person who was at first totally opposed recently visited the furniture works to see the new nave altar being oiled and to contribute money to making a matching lectern. Her delight was intense when she 'got what it was all about'. Our learning has been that different people need help to learn new things in a variety of time-consuming ways. Leading change involving the re-orientation of buildings usually draws out strong feelings for and against because our pictures of God and God's presence are being reformulated.

It's an essential part of my own leadership style to work with humour and conversation. However, when the normal church routines for deciding on the redevelopment of our building for mission today ran out of the goodwill of a vocal minority, we were thrown into the arms of the law. At this point the staff team and wardens really had to stop and pray and discern. Is it really essential for this church at this time to put itself through the sheer hard work and poor witness of going to law with members of the congregation over details of furniture layout? I had seen how a priest elsewhere had put up with the anguish of being opposed by various groups opposed to changing the inner design of a church much older than ours in order to have an appropriate space for the formation of a mutual rather than a hierarchical community. It seemed that although the law quite properly supports minorities, there was too much at stake for a critical mass of the congregation to simply capitulate.

So after much negotiation to prevent a hearing, the Chancellor of the diocese in gown and wig did preside over his court in the nave of our church. The preparation for the court cost us money, reputation and a great deal of emotional and practical energy. It felt like a very sad time but we made sure that we honoured the proceedings by careful attention to preparing papers and the arrangements in the building.

In the hearing itself the judge allowed people to give voice to a wide range of topics, from theories of church architecture and liturgy to minor complaints about personal behaviour. Throughout this stressful time I and other leaders frequently insisted and attempted to demonstrate how this was a test of our Christian identity. It would be useless to win the argument if the conversations and the ways of dealing with one another were not Christian.

Most of the people who were witnesses in court against the proposed changes have remained in the congregation and seem to have given up any resentment. Those who supported the innovation have offered friendship to those who opposed, rather than rejection. Frustratingly, that 18-month process meant that we lost a great deal of impetus for getting the work done and the building costs continued to rise, but we learnt so much about how to communicate and to disagree yet remain united. The outcome could have been a very different and negative witness without the various leaders 'getting it' that this was a test of our character and a chance to practise belief.

Holding theory and practice and reason and emotion in dynamic relationship is essential if the Church is not to be abandoned as having nothing unique to contribute or as obstinately fanatical and authoritarian. How would it be to rediscover Church primarily as a virtuous community? Its task as institution and local community is to bear witness in its daily operations and fulfilment of its mission to the love of God in its historical concreteness, conditioned by contingent historical particularities – partly just like the world and simultaneously completely different. As so many ecclesial systems have yet to learn, it's possible and profitable to reach decisions gradually and conversationally. Winning the argument is irrelevant unless the character of the exchange generates newness in which many people have an investment and reflects the courteous love of God revealed in Jesus.

2

God's people on the move

*Genuine innovation requires a new way
of seeing everything*

Let us never forget that love leads to wisdom. As the candle throws light on the surrounding world, so does the fire of love throw spiritual light on the universe and on ourselves. This wisdom is called transcendental because it transcends all reasoning and thinking and imagining. It is as far above all scientific knowledge as the light of the sun is above that of a tiny candle. We call this wisdom mysticism . . . the whole human family is called to mysticism.   (William Johnston 1999, p. 6)

Courageous catalysts, not superheroes

Western society seems in danger of polarizing so that the very privileged are increasingly separate from the poorest. The image of pixilating can be a way of describing our fragmented contemporary living that loses its sense of identity or coherence. In computer graphics and digital photography, to pixilate is to cause an image to break up into pixels, as by over-enlarging. Or it is used to describe blurring parts of a digital image by creating unclear, pixel-like patches that maintain the anonymity of the subject. So police sometimes ask the media to 'pixilate' the faces of people taken into custody.

Most churches are entangled in this society, but in the mess are also called to portray and strive for something more. The witness that the Church could be offering to a pixilating society is how to celebrate difference in unity and abundance in a time of austerity. Patterns of life as Church are constantly being born, flourishing and dying so that new ones can take their place. We can observe this phenomenon as, often with anguish and disappointment, congregations are grouped against their will to keep the system going a while longer. Increasingly, more localities are sharing the ministry of one stipendiary priest. It's routine to hear of clergy 'looking after' several parishes. At one conference, clergy were challenged, in a humorous spirit, to recall at one time the names of all the parishes for which they were responsible.

Pressure is rising for Anglican parishes to be radically re-invented. 'Fresh Expressions' has embodied a vital part of the necessary re-invention but dioceses continue naively and harmfully to appoint stipendiary clergy to churches that in their present way of being have no future.

In conversation with a provider of theological education, issues that arose included:

- Do we just create bigger 'ranches' to avoid the issue of closing buildings and starting new patterns?
- Are the parish clergy on the ground to bear the brunt of fulfilling continuing expectations concerning liturgy and buildings at the same time as trying to develop intentional communities for evangelism and discipleship?
- I have a decade and a half's experience of parish ministry. My impression since starting my role as educator and travelling more widely is that many clergy now are hugely more overstretched by two sets of expectations: first, right from the start of their training, their own personal, inner expectations of what they should be doing in ministry; second, the expectation – or perhaps only the hope – of their people, that existing 'services' (and pastoral care) will be maintained as further parishes are added.

There is no wonder that many do not have the energy or time to do more than lead communities that still vaguely hope the people 'out there' will 'come to us' and 'be like us'. I shall keep returning to the need for those in diocesan leadership roles to support the Church re-inventing itself at the local level and to promote training in the colleges and courses that sets up future ministers to be courageous catalysts, not superheroes.

Processes of grieving and lament, preferably with a consultant, have an important place before parishes can decide that sharing in God's mission takes priority over everything else. If local churches are to face the future through being Church differently, we shall need to discover new resources within ourselves (so that we can grow through the process) and we must be able to receive confident support from the diocese or region that is honest about the challenges and the resources needed in this emerging situation. Bishops and their teams owe it to parishes to make it a priority to encourage pioneering and to make available sophisticated processes for the management of change. In turn this must affect everyone as most church leaders already have full diaries in running the present paradigm.

As the hymns we choose testify to our belief about God, so does our public performance of developing discipleship and ways of being Church, locally and regionally. Discerning gospel-shaped practices for new circumstances is a continuing task, for which our primary resource is the Holy Spirit but also the full attention of those called to leadership. We have come to a new era. It is our choice whether simply to pretend this is not happening and keep on with our routines or, in the spirit of Christian pilgrimage, to find immense joy in letting go of past certainties and seek our future in God's purposes.

Ditching things that once seemed vital will be a prerequisite. Occasionally we remove from our wardrobe clothes we haven't used in the past year and take them to a charity shop. Similarly we could let go of the clutter of inherited church life. Indeed, we must face the fact that for many, and often for good reason, Christianity is a pernicious influence of which to be wary. This, combined with challenges associated with the Church's internal state of health as institution, provides an immense opportunity, long overdue, for living from a completely new perspective (Mark 1.15). Our priority now is to give time to listening more to Jesus and to society, and so to navigate a less grandiose and more open way of travelling. We must seize this opportunity with both hands.

Churches are rich in the underlying skills and attitudes of people just waiting to be noticed, appreciated and set free for the work of the kingdom. When we are regarded with deep respect rather than talked at or patronized, we can together be formed to show God's ways in the world.

Lists are plentiful of sustained woes and faults within the institutional Church. Without entering into detail here, I simply want to acknowledge some of the sharp systemic issues around clergy numbers, stress, depression, the constant increase in combining parishes, the dearth of real systemic and learning support especially for stipendiary clergy and parishes in new situations, too many buildings, insufficient administrative support, worries about finance, and the widening gap in our time between those who represent the Church and those who can no longer recite the Lord's Prayer with confidence. There are many, many parishes and leaders, ordained and lay, who are filled with passion for making Christ known through his Church. But as organizations, unless churches allot time and resources to attending to the systemic issues, ministers and communities committed to change will be exhausted and isolated.

I recognize that in holding together the paradox of hope and despair in churches at the moment it's easy to overbalance. The knife-edge balance between anxiety and the steady attempt to find new ways of being Church can be read, for example, in some entries in the Diocese of York Prayer Diary (October 2012):

- Please pray for the continued development of our deanery plan and for closer clergy and lay cooperation.
- Pray for a new vision . . . and thank God for a sense of growing and working together.
- Pray as we seek new initiatives.
- Pray for our priest-in-charge, who now has new pastoral responsibility for another parish.
- Give thanks for the success of Messy Church.
- Pray for those in a new combination of three former parishes.
- Give thanks for our small but faithful congregation.
- Give thanks for young men learning to follow Jesus.
- Pray for those in prison chaplaincy with new pressure on budgets.
- Pray for those called to lay leadership.
- Pray for all in this new formed Benefice and for all the parishes that will be joining.
- Pray for all who seek to meet the financial demands and maintain ancient and beautiful buildings.

Here is a snapshot of Church as it is now in many dioceses. The good signs are when communities themselves, and not just clergy, bear responsibility for reappraisal. However, the back pages of the *Church Times*, which carry advertisements for clerical and lay vacancies, still overwhelmingly look for a vicar who will sort things out rather than one who will help us all to move to a new way of seeing and being. Theology and common sense call us to look beyond clerical solo leadership. Incidence of stress and illness mean that although more exercise and praying, a better diet and a regular day off and retreat are ideal for leaders, the Church is in urgent need of honesty, trust in God and complex systemic support and management.

Institutionally, the days of the big idea, the expert or the diocesan plan are behind us. That's not to say that there is no need for creative and supportive institutional and episcopal response, but unless this is on a mutual basis it cannot deliver. A Church that is inherently relational will promote regular gatherings of laity and clergy to discern the future. Through worship and conversation, soundings can be taken and attention paid to many voices. If the Church's future shaping is not just the responsibility or interest of the clergy, there is urgency for individuals and teams to have forums that go beyond the formality of many synods. Everyone who cares needs to be carefully heard, rather than regarded as inadequate.

Among clergy and Readers I constantly hear questions such as, 'Where is this all going?' 'How much longer can we handle this?' 'Is this what God really wants of us, now, in this situation?' 'What is the connection between my ill health and the role I am now expected to fulfil?' 'Could I ever face becoming an incumbent again in these kinds of circumstances?' Systemic inadequacy is too often interpreted as personal ineptitude or failure.

From a Roman Catholic perspective, David Lodge in *How Far Can You Go?* (2011) taught us to ask, 'If this is the behaviour the Church is asking of us, what is the character of the God to whom we are invited to give our hearts?'

Often at great cost to themselves and their families, significant numbers of church people and leaders are giving sacrificially of their energy, thought and human qualities in taking stock and reconceiving ecclesial structures. Some dioceses are facing up to these issues and working hard to reshape expectations. They are recognizing that clergy and churches are experiencing distress and illnesses that are partly the result of forcing the old paradigm to work, at least on the surface. If for laity and clergy who give their all to be Church there is little joy or transformation, how can there be a joyful transformative proclamation of good news?

24

One report speaks of the present time as one of 'an unprecedented changing ministerial landscape' (Buxton 2012) in which some clergy and people are flourishing but many are floundering. Alyson Buxton, as rector, has resourced the South Wolds Group to move from 'pessimistic malaise' to 'living and developing the "now *what?*"' (p. 4). However, as she concludes, although personal courage and being the 'right-fit' are vital factors, there are systemic issues of managing and training for change as well as of language to be urgently addressed. Reports, as we shall explore, don't in themselves facilitate change in deep-seated practice.

At a recent clergy conference, participants expressed frustration that so many issues that have debilitated the Church for decades continue to do so. Some of the 'cries' of frustration were:

- Can we not manage appointments in a more professional manner? Not matching clergy carefully enough to situations results in huge distress for all concerned. We know this is difficult, but what a difference it would make even if archdeacons and bishops could be honest about the difficulties into which they are asking people to put their energy and spend time encouraging emerging possibilities. This would have to become a diary priority. Given the high incidence of stress in matching clergy to parishes, is it not worth introducing a review after eighteen months? Less harm might be done by admitting sometimes, 'we got this wrong; it's no one's fault, but this person is not going to flourish here'. What reorganization would be needed for diocesan staff members to have more time for these vital processes?
- Isn't it time clergy had sessions with a mentor as a matter of routine and not just in a crisis? This would mean a realigning of budgets but more fundamentally of attitudes that assume taking support is a waste of time or a sign of weakness.
- Can we have the courage to identify what has to be left behind to die? Which churches need to close? Which outdated agendas can we no longer resource? Who thinks that the ordination vows are sufficiently focused to tell clearly what the Church expects of various ministries?
- When will dioceses decide to spend money on giving parishes a share of an administrator so there could be pooled assistance with churchyards, building developments, legal issues, employment law

and finance? Or how can this partly be achieved through greater cooperation between parishes?

- When will the move from a serried hierarchy to an *episkope/koinonia* Church be seriously turned into new practices?
- What more help do clergy need to review goals and action planning as a result of Common Tenure? Who will be willing, and will make time, to provide it?
- Can we detach payment from commitment in the practice of ordered ministries? If we believe that all ministers are ordered together for the life of the Church, what difference in attitude and habits will this produce?
- How do we deal with disappointment – in ourselves as priests, in the churches we serve and in the wider community? A mutual Church will not hold some people to account unrealistically while others are passive. It is exhausting to keep finding the energy and persistence to subvert a culture of dependency as well as to deliver on so much that is expected or that I expect of myself.
- How can we learn from other churches more naturally? Instead of competition and concern with boundaries, how can we become naturally generous, open and vigilant for other churches?
- How many young Christians would seriously feel God calling them to manage the paradigm shift across several parishes within the present weight of heritage and individualistic culture?
- How do we productively engage with people in congregations so that they are fired up and not worn out? How do we balance the needs of an organization struggling to keep going with the needs of people to be nurtured in learning and prayer?

For an embodied Christian community life, mediating God's desire for the world, a new situation requires a fresh analysis and conceptualization of Church. It will need to be liberating, ecumenical, communal, holding in one movement both the temporal and the spiritual. Inevitably, we can recognize a complete mixture of hope and anxiety in the Church now.

- There are suburban parishes waking up to the vital need to nourish the faith and spirituality of their people but not wanting to drain the life out of people of goodwill.

- There are village churches really accepting that it's the whole Church, clergy and people together, who are called to be Church rather than 'going to church', and yet wondering how a tiny elderly congregation can rise to this.
- There are churches with long experience of 'being collaborative', recognizing the real pressure, illness and tiredness that has to temper their vision.
- There are experiments in extensive rural tracts, going beyond merely maintaining fragile and isolated congregations and unsuitable, expensive, cold buildings.
- There are clergy who, often against resistance and bewilderment, are facilitating church communities in evolving to meet the needs of a new era.

These are exciting and invigorating times for Christian communities that are ready for embracing change rather than fearing to be disloyal to our forebears.

Wisdom and virtues

The opportunity now is to let the Spirit lead us to find a wholeness and maturity that avoids a binary splitting of right or wrong, good or bad, catholic or evangelical, contemplative or charismatic. Our identity as Church must outpace our individual preferences. As a testimony against the individualism of society, we must learn to be gladly tolerant of the viewpoints of others, their ways of worshipping, learning and enjoying life. As a way of moving on from comfortable and well-worn but increasingly ineffective ways of Church, I propose we consider interweaving the Judaeo-Christian wisdom tradition with recent insights from a 'virtue ecclesiology' with especial reference to the work of philosopher Alasdair MacIntyre.

The Judaeo-Christian wisdom tradition and some liberation-focused feminist theologians advocate a holistic approach to wisdom, which combines knowledge, information-gathering, thinking, worshipping, praying, reaching healthy judgement and decision-making. Elizabeth Johnson, for example, describes wisdom (*Sophia*) as a passionate female street preacher, a prophet who cries aloud in the market place, as one who gives life. Sophia, beyond all gender stereotyping, loves, hates, demands and promises 'all in the interest of the ways of justice, truth and life, invoking Israel's unnameable YHWH' (Johnson 1998, p. 87).

Innovation within a relational culture

Grounded in and engaged with the cries of all who live with us locally and in society, Church is inherently relational, participative, resourced by but not dependent on clerical energy. Instead of diocesan initiatives and experiments, top-down, add-on and bishop-driven, now is the time for a huge shift of corporate consciousness. We are called to an evolution rooted in wisdom, formed in relationships empowering the people of God to live and move closer to God.

The sheer difficulty of managing and resourcing innovation cannot be overestimated. Attempts over recent decades to make a cultural shift through successive episcopally led initiatives have prepared the ground, but now it's time for a corporate, organic and relational wisdom to be articulated and owned. We must give thought and energy to release ourselves from restrictive habits. Our aim must be to create communities that are resilient yet sufficiently vulnerable not only to embrace change but to seek it and be ready to give wholeheartedly to wherever it leads.

Churches, like many organizations, live with the fantasy that a consultative report on a great idea, written by a group, will become reality just because it has been formally received. We can persuade ourselves that because a synod has debated and received it, the rest is automatic. The implementation of innovation is not something that churches tend to investigate thoroughly. We have not learnt from innovation failures in the past. To put it positively, the ways in which churches seek to make innovations need to be of the same character as the innovations themselves. So, for example, a vision that is inherently corporate cannot be implemented by an individual commissioned for the purpose. Bishops' staff teams are already multiply overwhelmed with managing what is. Innovation cannot be resourced on the back of diaries that are already full. The 2011 *Sustaining Leaders* report on the development of archdeacons identifies the high proportion of their time given to 'conflict management, interviewing, handling the relationships in a senior team, reviewing people's work, and supporting people through change' (Oxford Centre for Ecclesiology and Practical Theology 2011, p. 25).

On the whole, mainstream churches continue a long habit of investing money and time in stipendiary clergy, as the principal agents of ministry and mission. In these days of austerity it's a point of honour that numbers of diocesan resource personnel are kept to a minimum. Further, these are often deliberately linked with stipendiary shared posts because it's cheaper to pay a stipend than a salary and because it seems more genuine: 'These clergy know what it's all about because, like you, they're also running parishes.' Observation shows that as their energy is pulled in so many ways, they don't have time for more than maintenance in their home parish. In fact it would be better to deploy full time (for a period of, say, five years) those with a proven record in nurturing developments in local churches or with equivalent experience.

I write here with a degree of authenticity. As a diocesan and provincial officer over two decades, I've often been excited to be asked to lead initiatives that, in the end, have become a repetition of the past. After an initial period of recognition by some that this is a key advance for the churches, the dream fails because it's not possible for one person or even a small team to create lasting change in a complex and overworked institution. After a while some of the key players in a diocese with an investment in maintaining the predictable, safe business without malice can simply ensure that the church continues to invest in its normal business. It's not the hero's fault; it's not anyone's fault; it's just not an adequate pattern for implementing innovation. But nevertheless, we repeat the cycle.

Organizations are not naturally designed for innovation. However, those advocating radical experiments need the everyday work of the 'performance engine' (the everyday church routines) because it pays for the costs of innovation. Innovation is an emergent property of the relationship between the performance engine and teams dedicated to bringing about structural change. So the ordinary core business of churches is not the enemy but essentially the friend of innovation, and can in fact bring in changes within the slack of everyday business. They need to honour each other as partners.

Another key issue about innovation is that it cannot be planned on the same basis as continuing operations that are well defined, repeatable and predictable. Innovation, led by the Spirit, has the task of transforming what is standardized in the performance engine into new practices that carry the virtues and habits of gospel practice. This practice, as we have seen already, is always relational and demands the participation of many. What if we appreciate who is ready and open to change? What if a liberated and liberating approach has already caught the curiosity and creativity of many who desire a liberating future for the Church? What if we dare to encourage individuals and groups, already known to be experimenting with new aspirations and practices at the heart of the church, to see themselves as leading sideways, within the framework of mutual care and oversight of the wider Church?

An example of new practice is emerging from the Diocese of Lincoln (see Box 2.1). A Bishop of Lincoln, a few months into post, made it clear that the necessary implementation of changes identified

---

Box 2.1 Lincoln Diocese Central Services Review – implementation panels members needed

People from around the Diocese of Lincoln are being invited to put themselves forward for membership of nine panels which will see through the work recommended by the independent Central Services Review.

The review, which was considered at the meeting of Diocesan Synod in early October, received overwhelming support. Its 51 recommendations will now be implemented by the nine groups, each with a particular focus.

An appointments committee will oversee and review appointments to the panels, to ensure the right skills and expertise are represented on each, which will have oversight of strategy, the creation of a mission fund, governance, ministry development, discipleship, church buildings, a new way of collecting share, and worship enhancement and resourcing. It is expected that each panel would have no more than eight members.

'I am determined that I should not implement the Central Services Review report alone, but with the full support and involvement of people from around the Diocese,' said the Bishop of Lincoln.

'We are faced with an unparalleled opportunity to move the Diocese of Lincoln forward together, and to put in place the strategies which will help us to achieve the mission of the Church in the area.'

Those interested in joining the implementation panels can register their details on the diocesan website.

---

in a review would be a collaborative venture and not arranged either as a task for himself or as one that would be top-down.

Church exists to be a sign and mediation of God's integrating purposes for all Creation. Much of the time churches are in fact inhibiting this by too settled opinions and habits. Patterns of ministry must resonate with the purpose and virtues of Church that intends to be a re-presentation of Christian faith in the current age.

There are two particular pitfalls. One is to limit ourselves by recalling glories of the past and attempting to recycle the certainties that 'worked' in previous times. The other is to accept society's cynicism about faith and be reluctant to live joyfully and confidently in the presence and disturbance of God's call.

The Holy Spirit as comforter, midwife, guide, inspirer and challenger helps us embrace this particular critical time as a God-sent opportunity. In a postmodern world, opportunities will be met from many directions simultaneously. Conferences, publications and research projects such as the Durham University-based Receptive Ecumenism, led by Paul Murray, evidence local and courageous contributions to the restless search for new and sustainable forms of Church, learnt and received with integrity from other parts of the Church, in differing situations (Murray 2008).

A central pillar of our ecumenical, theological and scriptural enquiry into the Church's life today is located within the work of the Spirit, who inspires and corrects intentionally relational communities in their echoing of the mutual indwelling of the Trinitarian Persons. The Church's embodied gospel proclamation requires virtues and practices that are dialogical, involving all points of influence and partners. The voice of many participants must be welcomed, deliberately including those with whom, at one time, we have been in adversarial opposition, in terms of language or approaches to mission or priesthood. For Jesus, in proclaiming the kingdom to lepers, tax collectors and foreigners, the one thing excluded is exclusion itself.

3

A listening Church

*Learning from the wisdom of mystics and
organizational theorists*

Our whole world is in continued flux, and we have to use our
awareness consciously to keep abreast of the changes. The
excitement of realizing that the world is always new can lead
to real joy, but we have to be able to make the changes work
for us, and not continually defend against them. The world will
continue to change whether we like it or not.

(Oldham *et al.* 1988, p. 110)

Who is listening to us?

The Gospels show Jesus often ministering through conversation and
genuinely asking what someone required of him. Churches still generally prefer monologue to dialogue and competition rather than
engagement when it comes to gender, sexuality and deciding who
is a fit person to be ordained. Yet in a culture marked by overwork,
apart from those in dedicated care and counselling roles, friends and
family, few are prepared to listen attentively. Systemically, there is an
absence of being able to bear to hear those who are struggling both to
keep the Church viable and to re-imagine it at the same time.

Those pioneering radical patterns of Church or regularly overwhelmed by the multiple tasks they face need far more inclusion,
encouragement and care than they currently receive. Often there is
an appalling dissonance between those searching to find new ways
of being Church and those with particular institutional responsibility
for maintaining core business.

Seeking a holistic consciousness

Just as crusades can never be authentic advocates for the gospel, a Trinitarian way of being Church cannot emerge through the leadership of a linear hierarchy or a patriarchal culture. Clergy of my own generation have consistently overworked to hold everything together. In doing so, we must take responsibility for inhibiting the laity without realizing it, and failing to disclose God's gracious enquiring and appreciation of the contribution of all. In the late 1960s ordinands such as myself were inspired and rigorously formed in a sacrificial theology of the cross. To be personally aligned as a priest with the crucified Christ meant focusing intently on solo priestly ministry to the detriment of marriage, family and being in touch with contemporary culture. This is a caricature and there are many examples that offer a different picture, but the still prevalent texture of clerical dependency has its roots in a theology of a crucified Saviour, with little reference to the Holy Spirit.

Such personal dedication 'to be there for others' has brought a vital faith to many disciples and burned brightly within the ministry of many priests. Now there is urgent need of a rebalancing of our operational theology–practice to allow for the growth of entire Christian communities, identified as mutual 'one of another' relationship.

Technology is causing a revolution in the ways people juggle work and home. Some are flourishing through a merged lifestyle that combines within each day personal and public responsibilities. For others such an approach leads to the pressure of never having time off unless they are away completely from their normal environment. Some recently ordained are actively seeking to live more holistically and spontaneously, witnessing to the relational God rediscovered in the Trinitarian explorations of recent times. They might, for example, speak of their lives and those of their families as being 'informed' by their vocation to priesthood, but not as 'dominated'. It can no longer be assumed that spouses and families share the faith (or way of being Christian) with the ordained. Essentially today clergy (and other leaders) plan with spouses and family how to manage the whole of their lives so that their public role does not distort other relationships and vocations. This must be especially vital for those increasingly expected to take responsibility for overseeing multiple churches. It is not obvious that bishops and their staff teams have grasped this development and appreciated its important witness to the gospel the Church desires to proclaim.

Learning to be one of another

In local churches it is so often the case that too many worthy agendas are simply allowed to run without consideration of how much human resource is available. When a project is about to fail because it is under-resourced, who has the courage to let it go under? Most priests and lay leaders would overstretch themselves to ensure a particular project doesn't fail. That's understandable when we invest so much of our lives in the Church. The mistake is then to forget to review and enquire with others how not to get into that situation again. In other words, the whole Church has to act with a consistent mutual authenticity that echoes the Trinitarian God.

Listening and responding through intentional networking, both tangible and virtual, is essential. In Christian terms it's who we are, God's diverse people listening and engaging with one another, as the catholic (one and many) Church. As John's Gospel prologue, resonating with Genesis, reminds us, the light who comes into the world at the Incarnation is the same light that gives light to the world and the whole Creation (John 1.1–3).

So we can learn from a renewal of interest in integrationalist approaches to social understanding and learning. This is illustrated, for example, in a growing body of literature commending personal practices for balancing physical health, emotional balance, mental clarity and spiritual awakening (Wilber *et al.* 2008). The Church of England's *Formation for Ministry and a Framework for Higher Education Validation* (Church of England 2011) now probes specifically into how 'the curriculum integrates theory and practice and is flexible and responsive to changing needs'. College and course inspection looks for an integration of theory and practice that leads to theologically reflective and culturally aware practitioners. With regard to community life, corporate worship and ministerial formation, the Church of England expects students to:

- have an understanding of community life, including respect for issues of gender, ethnicity, disability and other matters of natural justice;

- learn on programmes that have clear connections with the institution's corporate worship and training in leading worship, including authorized and innovative forms and denominational worship as appropriate;
- experience suitable spaces for corporate prayer and worship;
- be stretched by a programme that enables trainees to deepen their understanding of the breadth of Christian tradition and its engagement with the world and to develop as theologically reflective practitioners and life-long learners.

It is impossible to forecast exactly what Church those now in training will be called to lead in even ten years' time – when so many stipendiary priests will have retired. There is a strong argument that for the sake of the health of the Church and its priests, the main criterion in training should therefore be to be formed as entrepreneurs. They will need to be committed to the relationality that can greet the unexpected no longer alone but essentially networked, receiving and offering resource according to their capacity. No one now should be accepted for training for stipendiary ministry who has not the potential to develop and flourish within such a culture.

Disciples of the psychologist Karl Jung have long spoken of the intuitive–holistic mode of consciousness. It may seem an alien expression and it is not so easy to explain, but it contains important insights for the Church's search to become more consciously connected with the whole of life.

While ordinary consciousness is concerned with external things and happenings, the 'other' mode of consciousness relates to bodily awareness and movement, feelings and physical capacity, affectivity and imagination. It is more akin to the apophatic, wordless tradition within Christianity. Active, verbal, objective, analytic, discussion-based modes of consciousness are concerned with the separate parts of things and how they might possibly connect.

There is considerable resistance to such approaches in society and Church as a sign of weakness or lack of resolve. Media commentators, after the 2012 Paralympic Games, were criticized for constantly asking successful athletes how they were feeling. But an intuitive–holistic mode of consciousness is an echo of Trinitarian aliveness as it expects to find meaning in the whole and in simultaneous, not sequential, process. So the dynamics and patterns of relating are vital experience for making intuitive, inspired guesses.

Other examples of working with an intuitive–holistic consciousness would be, first, Jean Piaget, who has shown how adults have often dismissed symbolic thought as childish. Second, Parker Palmer, who urges acceptance that excellent teaching cannot be reduced to technique; it comes from the identity and integrity of the teacher. Third, Charles Pierce encourages us to bridge the two ways of knowing: to appreciate affectivity and imagination in combination with our rational consciousness that works through deduction and induction. Theories of connectedness (for example Gestalt therapy, ecological and environmental studies and quantum physics) are increasingly appreciated for offering a critical threshold for personal and institutional living. Common sense, however, recognizes when to rely on Newtonian concepts, for stacking chairs perhaps, and when a quantum approach could be more generative in complex negotiations about the arrangement of the chairs for differing events. Finally, I value the report on recent research by Gerald L. Clore that emotions are deeply valuable in that they generate conscious thought to change oppressive situations:

> Such research is relevant in the present context because it indicates that rather than contaminating thought, emotion often stimulates thought, allowing for a revision of beliefs and intentions. Indeed if it were not for emotion, people might not think as they do. In the emotion of regret, for example, counter-factual thinking is stimulated concerning how a different decision might have led to different and more desirable outcomes.
>
> (Clore 2012, p. 216)

Art, poetry and literature, film and drama are increasingly recognized as ways of re-interpreting situations and attitudes and stimulating innovation. It's a priority now to build capacity in key leaders, such as archdeacons and training officers, for working with the intuitive mode of consciousness. Redressing the balance of an overemphasis on the rational and frequently dominating and adversarial approach is a top priority for diocesan and regional staff teams.

Moving to a new norm of consciousness that moves us beyond dichotomies and polar opposites towards integration and valuing intuition is painful, but essential and life-giving. It will not be possible without a reconceiving of roles and reshaping of work loads. The really hard question is: do we have the courage to let go of inherited expectations of leaders in order for this new culture to be born?

Listening to God: the mystics

There are clear links here to the mystical way, for example of Catherine of Sienna. She combined a great desire for individuals to know and love God with a deep concern for the Church. Her public ministry among bishops and monarchs was only possible through her intense spiritual experiences focused on the crucifixion and the Eucharist. Or again, echoing Colossians 1.27, the wisdom of Catherine of Genoa is summed up as 'My deepest me is God.' Julian of Norwich's physical–mystical connection with the Passion of Christ led to her receiving three wounds that could well serve the Church today: contrition, compassion and longing with all her will for God. Thomas Merton in his writing on contemplation invites the Church to fruitful action through self-forgetfulness and to the courage to face the sense of being untrue to the very things we most desire.

The challenge of listening and discerning has to move on from sheer stickability and managing old intractable problems. Dioceses could expect liberation and the release of new energy if they were to move out from formality and choose to carry the same virtues and habits as is expected of every local church.

> The mystics . . . talk of being ravished, seduced, of deep inner acceptance, total forgiveness, mutual nakedness, immense and endless gratitude, endless yearning, and always a desire and possibility of more. This is religion at its best and highest and truest. The mystics know themselves to be totally safe and completely accepted at ever deeper levels of trust, exposure, and embrace. Isn't this, of course, what all of us desire at our deepest level?
>
> (Richard Rohr in Finley *et al.* 2012)

God, who is everywhere, in every relationship, invites dioceses to take on a self-consciousness as an event or field of loving contact, enacted as a kaleidoscope of players. Instead of stability and uniformity as the norm – which is never the case anyway – dioceses, as fields of energy, could choose to regard movement as their identity. Appreciating the specialized function of intuitive consciousness, a corporate sense could emerge as always turbulently reconfiguring, through local congregations, incumbents, many clergy and leaders and teams in local churches, those who discern who will be ordained or licensed, those who support their formational processes and the bishops who hold overall responsibility for the flourishing and healthy ordering of the churches.

So the balance will be away from the overworking obsessed hero and towards patterns that allow for the development, inclusion and wholeness of all. Central to this project is the recognition that it is the whole Church that is called both to intensive relationship with God and to extensive relation with the whole of life. The entire *laos* (people of God) are gifted by the Spirit to make Christ present through making his Church present and operative in all the places where they are called to be light and salt.

However, the particular role of office-holders (vicars, curates and chaplains but also priest-missioners, development officers, stipended and non-stipended, as well as Readers and diocesan staff team roles) is a vital question to be explored. It's clear from an increasing volume of writing on this topic that reaching a generally satisfactory solution to this problem is proving elusive.

Listening to this place

Listening to Scripture and tradition, to the Spirit in worship, study and conversation and to God's call to work for that day when all things are fulfilled in Christ, requires that every church listens to its context. One of the essentials of incarnational Christian mission and ministry is to inhabit a place or group of places. The Judaeo-Christian wisdom tradition arises from God hearing the cries of people and communities, of joy, pain, despair and hope. To look closely at so many parts of Britain today, with reduced communal services and the consequent need for initiatives such as food banks and Street Pastors, is to recognize the prevalence of human isolation. Further, how can we say we know a community when people are living in flats with secured doors, gated communities with only a single access road, working long hours, absorbed in the upbringing of a young family, isolated through unemployment, ill health or caring for the chronically ill?

Part of the renewal of Church now must be rooted in our

understanding of God's redemptive presence and activity in every-thing. So when we say that God is Trinity we are suggesting that reality is in itself in some way communal and relational. We are being counter-cultural in an individualistic environment. To believe in God as Trinity implies that we will work with local communities respect-fully, openly, truthfully and with the capacity for self-criticism.

Navigating the complexity of local culture, speech and self-aware-ness requires emotional and spiritual intelligence. Emmanuel Y. Lartey, pastoral theologian, has identified a pattern in four stages of discovering and entering into awareness of the detailed networks of new social, cultural and spiritual environments (Lartey 2006, pp. 8–9):

- *Encountering the system* An initial stage of culture shock as we come into contact with the forces at work in a new place. This can involve a sense of confusion, rejection, regular illnesses, a sense of being helpless, bewildered or excluded, and a longing to become part of the normal life of the place.
- *Understanding the system* The stranger begins to have a more accurate cognitive knowledge of local educational, cultural and linguistic practices and customs. Vulnerability and anxiety associ-ated with arrival diminishes and we have a sense of being more in control. Awareness of people's expectations of the newcomer and the new person's own self-expectancy becomes clearer. Skills develop in navigating differences and in recognizing similarities with other places with which he or she has been familiar
- *Living within the system* At this stage cognitive and emotional intelli-gence begin to weave together as familiarity grows. The stranger has a sense of being able to participate in customs, activities and sports and enjoys being recognized, if only through his or her children.
- *Having (and using) authority within the system* Eventually we can start to explain how things work here, which links with the under-standing of others. We begin to understand the apparent contra-dictions and challenges. So we become more confident in taking our place, knowing our rights and assuming our responsibilities for the working of the system.

So Lartey very helpfully deepens our understanding of how a new-comer becomes integrated and can then generate change.

He commends an intercultural approach to living in particular places. This is grounded in the principles of contextuality, multiple perspectives and authentic participation. What becomes clear is that many arguments about ideas lose sight of the strength of social, cultural and historic influences. Learning to know and name the different perspectives in a single situation is a sign of a Church that listens accurately and respects – indeed, celebrates – diversity and conflicting voices. Only when this is the case will many other voices be drawn to take part.

Listening churches earn the right to say to people, 'Wake up! See this familiar place with new eyes. What difference can we now make together?' Jesus invited people to get a new way of seeing everything, to set out on new journeys, to be opened, to lose the disease of being deaf and dumb (Mark 7.34). Waking up is an image for asking deeper questions, beyond intellect but inviting the creative imagination to expect new life. Following Jesus means overcoming all that inhibits our lack of sight, hearing and speaking. Waking up means starting to listen, learning how to really see, discover and include the gifts of everyone, and especially appreciating the treasure of their particular cultures and traditions. All Church and theology is somewhere. Doing theology with sick and old people will take a different form from doing theology with managers or business people. In a mature Church, there is no theology, only particular theologies in earthen jars (2 Corinthians 4.7).

Listening to one another

Pressure on churches now requires that, using both spiritual resources and those of organizational theory, we learn more about honesty, vision, resilience, cooperation, practical wisdom, courage, compassion and conflict management.

Among those who lead in both paid and voluntary roles in churches, self-awareness must come as standard. Each person and group needs to be encouraged to practise the qualities and relationships of the interactive character of Church to which we aspire. As a leading practitioner in systemic change, Bill O'Brien summarized, 'The success of an intervention depends on the interior condition of the intervenor' (O'Brien n.d.). Those whose task it is to promote communities of mutual animation (Romans 12.5) will include the following in their questions for regular self-review: 'Who am I in this situation?' 'What difference does it make when I act or speak or when I am present or absent?' 'Am I acting within the flow of what I have agreed with colleagues as our aligned purpose and ethos?' 'Do I recognize the difference between myself in role and myself as a human being?'

Action-logics

The potential of giving time to such searching processes as routine is summarized and expounded notably by Bill Torbert (former Professor of Management, Boston College) and associates. Their passion is for organizations to thrive through learning excellence in communication, interpersonal effectiveness and team-building. We may be familiar with the language of traits and capabilities but Torbert uses the term 'action-logics' (Torbert *et al.* 2004). This may be puzzling at first, but I believe it is one way of recognizing what we hadn't seen in ourselves, rather as a fish doesn't notice the water in which it swims.

The value of this kind of systemization of human development (illustrated in Box 3.1 on p. 44) is that it offers us a mirror or a friend to help us bring our actions into awareness. So, for example, if we begin to notice for the first time the effect of our loud voice or forceful personality, we can dare to develop new ways of being with others that are more mutual. But such discoveries increase our levels of vulnerability, and such development work needs mentors and safe spaces that at present are not routinely expected of those in church leadership. It is, I believe, an important route for the growth of Christian community practice. With support, we can choose and create ways of becoming conductors of the spirit of a more relational Church.

Bill Torbert's professional work is to reflect on tough decision-making in business. This involves creating a balance between getting work done, caring for human safety, acting ethically, holding conversations between those in responsible positions and maintaining the reputation of the company. Torbert and his associates propose a systemic way of understanding these dynamics, 'Triple Loop Feedback' (Torbert *et al.* 2004). They describe Single Loop Feedback as getting a task done on time and efficiently; this clearly has an important place in any community, system or institution and is about observing our behaviour. Double Loop Feedback arises when we are confronted with new choices that require us to adjust our initial structure or behaviour: 'The situation has changed. What shall I do in order that the end result is not just efficient but effectively fitting with the goals of our community or institution?' Torbert describes how efficiency in a task can end up being ineffective if we fail to see or respond to our surroundings and to other people who are investing energy or even their lives into a project.

A very primitive example would be starting to clear out junk from the church boiler-house and considering hiring a skip and sending it all to landfill, so creating more space and less of a fire hazard. A second thought, in consultation with others, would be to discern what would be useful to keep (maybe a huge cross made by a former member of the church that once a year, at Easter, is invaluable), even if it does take up room. Also, Second Loop Feedback would discern what might be recycled. This would take time and effort but would be a sounder ecological approach, appropriate to the virtues and habits of Church.

Triple Loop Feedback goes beyond action and strategy to 'attention itself'. Torbert draws out the possibilities for an enterprise when we start to work counter-intuitively through a transforming power that assumes mutuality. For this to develop we have to disengage ourselves from being identified with current structures, strategies or ways of working. There can be strong resistance when we feel we are losing our identity until the realization dawns that this is the way to find a deeper identity that is real, going beyond roles, masks and self-image. We are invited to become more present to ourselves, more awake and confidently aware of other aspects of situations and choices. It takes time and concentration and respect for others' learning – not just getting jobs done.

There are many scenarios for churches where such frameworks open our awareness. The invitation is to realize our limitations when we work in isolation or without awareness, imagination or sufficient information. Once we see the point we have to make it part of our working routine to combine rather than separate effective working and imagination. However, as Wilber *et al.* (2008) describe in detail, to improve the quality of our awareness requires constant practice. We shall only be bothered with this if we accept how limited is our ordinary attention, even when we're deliberately focused and alert. Torbert identifies and explores with illustrations four areas of awareness to enhance adult learning and organizational life:

1 *Outside events* Results, assessments, observed consequences of behaviour, effects on the environment
2 *Our own sense of our performance* Behaviour, skills, ways of acting, deeds, in the course of enacting our work

3 *Action-logics* Strategies, plans, ways of getting things done, schemes, typical ways of reflecting on performance

4 *Intentional attention* Supervision, the awareness that comes through being really present, vision, intuition, aims, our own performance.

A key part of the analysis of Torbert and associates (reflected on over time) proposes seven modes (action-logics) in which people regularly operate, through a spectrum of increasing sophistication and sensitivity to situations. Of course, no one occupies just one place. The issue is which are within our range of operating. They are labelled as opportunist, diplomat, expert, achiever, individualist, strategist and alchemist. This schema is a reminder of the complex motives that underlie all our practice and also of the possibility of us outgrowing our original intentions and limitations and deepening our awareness and intentions. The present moment is what really matters. What is our practice *now*?

Each action-logic or stage of development is a coherent and internally consistent belief system that describes how its proponents are likely to think, feel and behave in various life situations. Box 3.1 overleaf describes seven action-logics of increasing complexity, each one more effective, insightful and integrated than the previous one. Each of the action-logics also has its own strengths and vulnerabilities and there is no suggestion that as leaders we simply occupy one of the logics to the exclusion of the others.

Few of us would not aspire to becoming an alchemist, who has grown into a wise knowing beyond mere expertise. The aspirations of alchemists in ancient myths were not only about turning base metals into gold but also influencing the constellation of the heavens. At some time, I hope, we all have the experience of bringing people and events together in such a way that there is a transformation that none of us could have imagined.

To seek transformation in ourselves and our capacity to enact the values of integrity, mutuality and sustainability requires that we need support to notice, name and make choices. Torbert proposes an action-logic sequence to encourage our transformation, which he emphasizes is never as mechanistic or smooth as its representation in the developmental map might seem at first sight.

This framework invites us to become more aware of the inconsistencies and self-limitations in our performances and the ways we could grow into a greater consciousness. For churches to develop

Box 3.1 Action-logics: a summary of Bill Torbert's research conclusions

- *Opportunists*, who focus on what they can take from a situation and sit light to accountability. This logic is based on unilateral power that works on short time frames, grasping opportunities and dealing with crises to the near exclusion of all else. Acting in time is essential in order to 'win'. Opportunists don't take account of how their actions now will impact on their relationships with others in the future. Their key questions is, 'How can I get what I want at any cost?'

- *Diplomats*, who work on the surface, seek approval and are company workers. The diplomat works from his or her sensed performance territory of experience and concentrates on self-mastery to be effective. Imitating the attitudes and performance of higher-status group members, this action-logic focuses on routines, detail, punctuality and short to medium time scales. The diplomat's key question is, 'What is expected of me?'

- *Experts*, who seek to solve problems efficiently and be recognized for having unusual skill. The primary reality is the strategic territory of experience and the focus is on learning a discrete discipline. Six months to a year is their favourite time line for accomplishing projects, and efficiency is the watchword. Their key question is, 'What is the best/right way of achieving this?'

- *Achievers*, who work for long-term goals in practical matters, initiate change, respond to feedback but are low on self-awareness. Most workers transform themselves towards expertise, but around just 40 per cent move to the achiever action-logic. Their time frame is one to three years, within which they learn to juggle planning, performance and assessment of outcomes. Some immediate 'wins' are balanced with the longer-term, agreed, efficient outcome that satisfies the client or constituency. They are different from experts as they understand that they need to bring the team with them rather than just getting the job done. They take feedback – but only if it is in line with their own beliefs and values. They can be a little parochial, looking for best practice within their organization. Their key question is, 'How can we achieve this, in the usual way that we work here?'

- *Individualists*, who are the entrepreneurs, moving beyond convention, increasingly aware of having impact and preferring creativity over imposed objectives. The path towards this action-logic is likened to a reflective and confusing somersault through our own history and the growing recognition of choice. Something of us has to break or unravel and become re-formed. There is an obvious parallel here with the dark side of the spiritual journey, articulated by John of the Cross and many others. The emerging individualist holds together past and present and conflicting emotions, and sees time as fluid and containing times of particular intensity; she will notice and be interested in her own and others' forms of self-expression, seeks independent and creative work, is more attracted by change than by stability, is disinclined to judge or evaluate, influences more through paying attention to new ideas and patterns than by advocacy, can become a maverick, and starts to be more aware of how she is present to others and the impact this may be having; she can be inhibited in decision-taking. Individualists realize that there is no right way and that each person's point of view is valid, but this can cause them some anxiety as it may mean that finding a way of leading a task or team becomes much more complex. Their key question is, 'What's your take on this?'

- *Strategists*, who excel in conflict, operate out of wisdom beyond rules, live with paradox, can be present in a variety of ways, are self-aware and know the temptation to power. In this action-logic there is an eagerness to challenge others into joining in the leadership process. Very attuned to the developmental process, the strategist welcomes the combination of a growing individualism in the context of mutual relating. He is keen for others to develop through experience, mistakes and a growing alertness. Strategists recognize the importance of Triple Loop self-correction and the ultimate value of interdependent working. Whatever their assigned role in an organization, those working from the strategist action-logic are leading by living with unresolved tensions and by framing new opportunities. Their lightness of touch, humour, sensitivity, holistic way of living and world view also includes a natural concern for self-care and an individual's personal spiritual journey.

- *Alchemists*, who, through profound experience, emerge largely free of ego drives, make interventions that reframe situations, enjoy ambiguity, metaphor and symbols. This has been summarized as the intuitively appealing idea of keeping our souls and ideas fresh. Torbert approaches the description of this rare action-logic through accounts of a few who, through a lifetime's confrontation of their limits and painful transformation, have discovered 'the secret of timely and transforming leadership' (Torbert *et al.* 2004, p. 192).

practices of mutuality and cooperation, finding supportive and challenging ways to see ourselves in context is vital. Watching out for logs in the eyes of others is our temptation, and it would be all too easy merely to diagnose where our colleagues fit on this scheme. Knowing the love of God for our broken selves can give us courage to reflect where we would position ourselves within such a matrix. With the support of others we can then choose to see ways of reframing our practice within the teams to which we contribute and to build capacity into the whole. Looking beyond the linear presentation of Torbert's analysis can open to us the parts that cause some real unease as well as the parts that seem to say, 'I could be like that.'

Initially it can seem hierarchical, with those advocating such a framework placing themselves at the top, but the higher action-logics are attracted to difference and mutuality, a network view of life rather than a hierarchical tree-like view. There are clear advantages when individuals and groups confidently practise a constant interweaving between being productive and being self-evaluating. Churches that should easily grasp this, through the legacy of wisdom and mysticism, instead often present as in denial or having all their memory space taken up.

A diocese that promotes listening

Those with enhanced public roles in the Church have a special task of rekindling hope and energy while being able to hear and bear the painful tensions and realities being experienced by local people and ministers. Whenever bishops and archdeacons are with clergy and parishes, they need to recognize that, 'Yes, we've been through changes before, but this is an especially tough and holistic one and we're not in denial about it. We know now that there are no quick fixes or universal remedies, but we are giving primary energy and thought to encouraging and creating ecologies of learning for the sharing and critiquing of initiatives.'

In the light of a relational understanding of Church in which everything is connected, a situation where clergy and other leaders are overwhelmed by their roles and expectations is a pain that belongs to everyone and needs to be recognized as such. Increasing numbers of conscientious clergy are reported to be in need of time out and therapy through becoming exhausted, disillusioned or seriously ill. Individual pastoral care and counselling for those who are 'stressed' may be required short-term. A truly collegial Church will be pro-active in reflecting with all concerned, in fostering networks and in identifying the resources to support those who are on the frontier of major change and shifts in expectation.

A diocese that provided regular supervision for its clergy would be making a sound investment. New and hard-won insights would promote a cycle of change in all with whom that diocese worked. Pastoral support alone, when we struggle with difficult situations, is a reminder of the inadequacy of the regime of simply patching up men to return to the same trench warfare during the First World War, so that at any cost the war might be finished for the sake of future generations (see Pat Barker 1991).

In whatever clusters work locally, there need to be routine gatherings of everyone with a key role or interest. Through worship, silence, imaginative study of Scripture such as *lectio divina* or other participative process, and sharing food, conversations can take place to build personal confidence and competencies for churches to:

- excel at seeing themselves as part of a whole, rather than just isolated parts, in support of fundamental innovation and change. This links to developing past achiever action-logic (adult development is the best way to shape leadership culture and thus organizational forms);
- become instinctively and joyfully collaborative across boundaries to engage all relevant stakeholders and their interest effectively, create healthy social networks and find new practical and emotionally healthy ways of working;
- move from problem-solving to conversation, exchanging, encouraging and testing new patterns of Church, evoking inspiration and creativity between churches and confidently moving towards possibility and in the process telling the story to whoever will listen.

The style and quality of these events will need to be a high priority for those responsible, with the courage to take feedback and listen and respond to it. To advocate and invite people to such gatherings in the first place, we could be saying:

These gatherings need to be designed so that local churches together become learning communities, created through conversations of hope, and working with other participants on real issues and relationships.

In particular, such events could offer participants the opportunity to:

- be present to one another in a spirit of mutual love;
- become more skilled at helping individuals and teams work more effectively and collaboratively within and across systems;
- discover practices and learn from one another how to transform challenges into opportunities for innovation and growth;
- face up to and learn from situations that haven't worked out well;
- enhance their ability to inspire and engage others in initiating and facilitating change;
- share hope among one another, through the Holy Spirit, for the present and future of their church and its ministries.

The purpose of these gatherings will be to listen to one another and to share the 'sources' of our leadership, in whatever way we are currently called to participate. Throughout the Church this culture is growing, as for example when recently in the Durham Diocese almost 100 people took part in an event called 'Reaching out to Communities'. Participants will go away with a renewed understanding of how they can facilitate change, both within their organizations and in their personal lives.

Such an approach would be exploring personal discipleship, collaborative enquiry and a holistic, mutual perspective for sustaining profound innovation.

In particular, participants could expect to:

- discover a more coherent picture of the results they most desire to create individually and collectively alongside a realistic assessment of the current state of their church today;
- understand how the way they live as a corporate body shapes their practice, and how to recognize and make a difference within those structures;
- expand their capacity to identify and improve on good practice;
- become more able to discern mutual purpose and shared commitment;

- explore underlying beliefs and assumptions and their impact on their capacity to be Church and to be leaders;
- learn to balance and integrate intuition and rational understanding;
- learn how to facilitate conversations that promote learning and collaboration;
- start to operate from their deepest source in God.

Such an approach would require a diocese to focus its energy on resourcing and funding the development of laity and clergy for innovation.

Importantly, not only the local church but the entire institution must take its part in communicating the gospel through intentional practice. Crucially, the institution is always at the service of practice and not the other way round. Fortunately, within Anglicanism there will always be those, often so-called 'lay' people, who will subvert any attempt by clergy or administrators to lose sight of core practices. So, for example, when one group becomes engrossed in liturgical correctness, others will rebalance with pastoral care; those who focus on reshaping buildings will need to be persuasive and willing to negotiate to win sufficient consent.

Listening bishops

Accepting the call of God and the Church to the role of bishop requires a willingness to hold together past and current practices of Church with newly emerging ones. In *Parish Priests* (Greenwood 2009) I recorded some of the tensions and conflicts that exist in bishops' diaries. Conversations with bishops who are retiring can reveal a frustration that the very gifts and insights they believed they were bringing to the role have been drowned under the weight of conflicts or struggles simply to maintain the existence of the Church. Even in a neo-atheistic culture, being a bishop in England still carries a different set of public expectations from those in other provinces.

Bishops generally exercise a unifying, generalist, conservative function, seeking to be equally understanding and available to all.

The accumulated weight of responsibility for the health of a diocese combined with a sense of powerlessness and the demands of instant communication lead many to work too many hours in each day and too many days in each week. There often seems to be a spectrum that ranges from the holy, scholarly and non-interventionist to the pace-setting, micro-managing and project-leading bishop. Of course that's too simplistic, but it is an invitation to rethink how the Church can most effectively deploy its bishops. If we can be clearer about our need of them now, in this present moment, we might have the courage to revisit the practice of the role.

Every month produces yet another book on how to be a parish priest in the present climate. So, for example, we look for pioneer priests who will bring a fresh approach to evangelism and social action. What we most need are pioneer parishes. I am convinced that the shaping of all public ministries can no longer be practised in isolation. It's always an ecclesial issue: what can the Church expect of Christian communities of the baptized and their resources or animators, Readers, priests, bishops and deacons?

Also we can be too preoccupied with the views, personality and background of our bishops. I've worked in dioceses expecting a new bishop where everything is in freeze frame until we know what the new bishop 'prefers'. Just as we no longer expect the solo parish priest, the mono-episcopal style of leading a diocese is no longer fit for purpose. It's the radically relational ordering together in *episkope* (see p. 9) that can help us most. What do we now require in those called, for the present moment, to occupy that episcopal chair in relation with everyone else?

In this critical time, the primary task of the bishop is to demonstrate and promote various kinds of listening:

- Listening to God's dynamic ordering of Creation and Church through Scripture, Eucharist, worship, prayer, study, reflection, silence and conversation is the non-negotiable heart of being Church. Perfunctory prayers at meetings, to save precious time, make a powerful statement about the Church's virtues and practices.
- Listening to the detailed difference between localities, rather than perpetuating a territorial approach, arises from a Trinitarian consciousness of God in the unity of difference.
- Listening to churches that are giving time to innovation is a priority.
- Spending significant time in parishes that are pioneering and filled

with a blend of confidence, apprehension and hope is vital.

- Listening to one church listening to another and learning more from and between contexts is to be preferred to sending out messages from the centre about practices and goals.

Bishops and their teams need completely to re-examine how they match clergy to increasingly complex tasks. Once a good enough match is made, bishops bear the responsibility – along with the diocese as a whole – for safeguarding clergy through the provision of mentoring, networks and every conceivable way of offering support. In return clergy must give up the spirit of independence and isolation. Behind all of this, bishops need to help their diocese re-imagine what God is calling Church to be today. This process involving the skills and care of all could lead to a leaner, healthier, more robust and Christian Church locally and institutionally. Only when we know how the diocese in its variety of contexts now senses God's call can we know what kind of bishops we require and who can best fulfil the role.

Instead of recruiting women and men who will be expected to overwork in order to maintain the inherited spirals of expectation, a virtuous Church will promote networks of consultancy and discernment. We must see how many of our 'failings' are relational and systemic. Instead of spending first-aid time with parishes and clergy who seemingly can't crank the handle vigorously enough, bishops need to understand and encourage ways of re-inventing Church. This also means guiding synods and staff teams to make wise decisions about supporting change, spelling out that this has to be and that every care will be taken of those on the frontier.

Stephen Pickard exposes the flaws of an individualistic understanding of ministry. He draws out the joy of membership of *the other* within the body of Christ. His concern for the retrieval and release of God's energy within the whole Church and world finds its source in a ministerial dynamic that is fully relational, so that neither ordained nor other ecclesial ministries can be what they are *without the other*: 'Such is the delicate ecology of order within the ecclesia. Where this works well the praise of God is released and its effects magnified in an outflow of witness and joy' (Pickard 2009, p. 166).

4

Learning together

Choosing cooperation rather than competition

Do you know of small efforts that grew large not through replication, but by inspiring each other to keep inventing and learning?   (Margaret Wheatley and Deborah Frieze 2011)

Learning through networking

There's an acronym, WEIRD, standing for Western, Educated, Industrialized, Rich and Democratic, that reminds us of how most of the world takes a completely different view of things from ourselves. 'Will my child have anything to eat today?' is for many people, globally, more important that the effective functioning of the Church. Often the world can show the Church just how to practise that catholic, common, shared life demonstrated by the gospel. One such case is innovation in the global field of poverty alleviation, where small local efforts are moving trans-locally through networked relationships.

The following account is not about Church but is a reminder of the light that fills the whole world (John 1). It is without doubt an example of the Spirit at work among people and could carry over analogously into the re-imagining of Church.

In Joubert Park, South Africa, faced with continuing and immense problems including drugs, prostitution, child rape, unemployment, lack of education or health care, typical of so many other places, the community lost faith in professional problem-solvers. Instead of depending on them they took seriously words of Archbishop Desmond Tutu: 'We are bound together by our caring humanity, a universal sense of *ubuntu* . . . we are created to live in a delicate network of interdependence' (Wheatley and Frieze 2011, p. 84).

The local slogan became, 'Go inside. Start anywhere. Follow it everywhere', as a group of photographers, struggling to make a living, hit on the idea of actively photographing crime as it took place in Joubert Park, a tensile and mistrustful place. The results of purpose-fully photographing crime led to the police being able to have good evidence to intervene effectively. Gradually the level of crime dropped so that secure, ordinary life could emerge. Joubert Park became a more stable place to live, where simple local initiatives led to safe play areas for children, places for young people to gather and talk in safety, a progressive green initiative that produces healthy food, the recyc-ling of water and waste and eco-friendly building.

'Go inside. Start anywhere. Follow it everywhere', as an attitude, led from a small group of courageous photographers working out how they could have a livelihood and at the same time draw atten-tion to real crime taking place, leading to a productive environment for every member of the community. No one planned this process. A local initiative that paid attention to the intricacies of a place led to the transformation of despair into hope. Margaret Wheatley's and Deborah Frieze's *Walk Out Walk On* (2011) contains many examples of communities moving from limited beliefs and activity through discovering latent gifts to meet seemingly unsolvable problems.

Paying attention to the intricacies of a situation was the start. An original idea grew into something else. As more people and places join an experiment, larger-scale change and hope emerge. As one place connects with others and finds new possibilities, pioneering methods are scaled across and become accepted, normal and satisfy-ing. This requires an end to competition and the embracing of coop-eration: in the Church's terms, catholic collegiality. And of course in a Church that continues to work hierarchically this example is too loosely formed in itself but holds an imaginative possibility if given breathing space and support in the catholic ecology of a diocese.

No general path exists; there is only the rediscovery and iden-tifying, over time in particular places, of the character and task of Christian communities and their institutions. 'Go inside. Start any-where. Follow it everywhere' has a lot to show us about scaling across or learning in humility and joy from the pioneering of others. It's a frequent problem for churches living competitively rather than col-legially that we can't receive from one another in generosity. The invi-tation from the account of Joubert Park is to enjoy working through exchange and mutual concern, especially as we come to terms with the fact that the abundant resource we have is one another.

An example of unexpected cooperation between parish church and local shopping centre (which is described more fully on page 138) again has possibilities for scaling across in other contexts. In a suburban seaside parish with no obvious public meeting place a small shopping centre has discovered new possibilities. Delicate negotiations between a priest colleague and a coffee shop proprietor led to a new vision of how to use the space at Christmas and for a community gathering where everything was provided free, releasing a nascent energy and confidence. There is a particular capacity for the Anglican Church in the UK to become such a catalyst without taking over or manipulating the dynamic. Similar examples will no doubt come to mind in the experience of readers.

Learning through conversation

The discipline known as *Appreciative Inquiry* (AI), as featured in the work of Diana Whitney, Sarah Lewis, Jonathan Passmore, Stefan Contore and others, focuses on transforming a community's self-image, building relationships among diverse and even conflicted groups and creating a positive culture (Whitney and Trosten-Bloom 2003; Whitney *et al.* 2004; Lewis *et al.* 2011). AI can also be instrumental in moving us from the 'discussion' (literally 'cutting in pieces') of 'problems' to the drawing out of wisdom in conversation around the experiments and experiences we all bring, leading to a sense of hope and encouragement. The mood of AI can best be portrayed as working Spirit-fully, appreciatively, curiously, generously, playfully and irreverently (Lewis *et al.* 2011, p. 117). AI can transform gatherings for the mutual support of church leaders away from rehearsing seemingly intractable problems. Instead of objective criticism and diagnosis, it invites participants to ask unconditional questions that strengthen the capacity of people and groups, inviting the sharing of competencies, stories and dreams.

The vital ingredient of being fully present, on a personal and communal level, is now established in many of the disciplines of business leadership, education and psychotherapy, and Christian spirituality. Nothing of great consequence can happen until participants dare to be in touch with their deepest source in God. When groups move from mechanistic planning and begin to operate from a real future possibility, they discover a new kind of social field that is characterized by:

- its quality of thinking, conversation and common action, so that there is a connection with a deeper pool of creativity and wisdom that overtakes previous patterns;
- a continuing rippling out of this experience that leads to previously unknown and fruitful ways of working together;
- heightened individual energy and awareness, a deepening of authenticity, and a more focused sense of direction and significant accomplishments;
- a realization that crises can't be solved by repeating the past or staying as we are, but only by individual and collective transformational change;
- a sense of being part of something already happening, through letting go of the old body of institutionalized collective behaviour in order to meet and connect with the presence of previously unconsidered possibilities;
- a willingness in a critical situation for leaders to learn from the highest possible future, rather than repeat what used to work;
- recognizing as 'leaders' any who take part in creating change or shaping their common future, regardless of their formal position in the institution.

A group of parishes has a strong connection with an art college and annually has been delighted that students of all ages have exhibited their assessed work for a week in the nave. There has been a mutual learning between older members of the congregation and the students. A great deal of the practical brokering of this event has been taken on by David, an early-retired manager. He would say, 'I know nothing much about art but I have gained a great deal through asking questions and finding how delighted were the exhibitors to explain their vision and techniques.' Equally, we know that the students have enjoyed speaking with David. He showed them that Church need not be formal, stuffy and disapproving but, rather, welcoming and genuinely interested in the whole of life. Courage and willingness to take risks are required to be a mediator of Christian identity, however obliquely and diffidently.

Being present to one another

'Presencing', working from the future as it emerges, demonstrates our openness to God's inspiration as well as offering our imagination and love to help to bring the future into reality now. Organizational theorist Otto C. Scharmer (2009) has systematized the benefits of being consciously present to our tasks and colleagues:

1 *Exploring the future* How can we make the biggest difference? What are the best questions we can ask? How can we reframe or re-imagine it, re-invent ourselves institutionally and personally, in an evolutionary process, a whole different way to act as change agents, bringing forth a Church profoundly different from that of the past – involving head, heart and hand?
2 *Redesigning* We make a start by designing a first idea and exploring the future by trying things out, integrating head, heart and hand, living examples, navigating between dangers, integrating different forms of intelligence, connecting to inspiration across the widest canvas, listening to the context, creating real places for future possibilities.
3 *Performing* We need to make it part of what we do, shaping something that empowers, part of a web of relationships, of value for those who need our work, learning, innovating, changing and relating local to the wider realm.

In my own experience, learning eventually not to rush but to take time for prayer, conversation and refining possibilities diminishes the sense of panic or the attitude that we have to work hard to please God. When a group can risk being fully present, looking for the crack where the light is showing through, they move beyond efficiency to a transforming power that is an expression of a deep mutuality.

Learning in vulnerability

When Church is an event disclosing something of the mystery of Trinitarian love, a unity in difference, there will be evidence of the expectant courtesy that characterized Jesus' way of relating. Whether in supervision of colleagues, reviewing our team or assessing our own performance, seeking the goal of being intimately present to the whole field of relationships is a habit to be desired. Practically, this means attempting to hold together four areas of experience simultaneously: everyday events; results and effects; our own sense of how we have performed in a situation; and awareness of the field of people and systems and how present we have been.

When we are speaking of a community that echoes God's being, we have to live with the not-yet character of Church. This holds in tension resurrection life, as a force already let loose in history to display the radical dignity of every human being, along with the Church's regular disfiguring and sinful ways of relating.

It takes prophetic courage to risk being open or vulnerable in places where institutional life usually invites formality, competition and objectivity. For example, the most articulate of laity who hold great responsibilities in work can be inhibited sitting round a table at a Bishop's Council. The challenge of 'presencing' carries with it questions about the way those with high profiles in a diocese can perceive how hard it is for others to participate and to make changes to the culture.

I know what a difference it can make when planning meetings begin in prayer, for example in the spirit of Mark Yaconelli's Ignatian-inspired *Contemplative Youth Ministry* (2006). A genuine encounter with God and with others can give a creative focus to conversation and planning. The important learning is for local churches to move on from prescriptive programmes, learning instead to recognize and break the cycle of fatalism. A leader helps people to realize and believe that they can shape their own future.

Exuberant and convivial churches need to exchange unconscious habits of hoarding resources or being competitive for habits characterized by sharing life stories, recognizing the way many people contribute to successes and work as a community tackling tough questions. In this way the appreciative and presencing process itself is the pioneering journey towards a church with a future, attractive yet unknown. *Some* of the following characteristics can be found and nurtured in *a few* people who can be pioneers:

- a belief that all God's people matter and can make a difference;
- a respect and care among people of diversity;
- a place where in courtesy we speak directly;

- conversations and reflections where God and Jesus and the Spirit are spoken of in a natural way;
- worship in which different paths to holiness are regarded with respect;
- gatherings where people's stories are heard and attract attention;
- attitudes of respect so that the locality in which the church is set is not a problem but a place full of God's activity;
- a community where people support each other in praying and meditating on Scripture, in different ways;
- a spirituality in which God is known in ordinary things;
- meetings where there is humour and laughter as well as lament and tears;
- a plan for mission and evangelism where there is an expectation that people of varying temperament and capacity can be witnesses, leaders and animators;
- a setting/community where we continually grow in our conversion to Christ and where we are merciful with each other in our imperfections.

And of course we live in the 'now but not yet' of reality. We could equally make a list of the opposite of each of these points that truly inhibit the practice of Church. Each has its counter-side in Christian communities that have become timid, unfriendly, inward-looking and frozen in a past form. When we conspiratorially sing, 'Be still, for the presence of the Lord is moving in this place', it's important to remember how the Holy Spirit is as much challenger as comforter to the people of God.

Learning to be a mutual Church

For communities to learn the habits of risk, uncertainty, mutuality and vulnerable love requires care in the discernment of who might become wise leaders, including priests, within our churches. Across a spectrum of temperaments and ways of viewing life, we need those who will be suspicious of adopting pre-packaged programmes that are unrelated to context. Rather, we need to discern sufficiently those who are growing into maturing in Christ, to resource churches in recognizing wise judgements, priorities, decisions and actions.

In many disciplines we can no longer trust a linear relationship between theory and practice, assuming that one or the other will always come first. We need to be able and willing to live with an uncertain interplay between them that goes beyond rationality. Christian priests and colleagues will need a wisdom that will promote authentic ways of being Church in the unknown territories of the twenty-first century. Churches have to learn how to weave together Scripture – with all its interpretations – and twenty centuries of experiments in how to be Church, within the contemporary world's many contexts. This process for churches requires immersion in God's life, so that we have a rock to stand on in complex and demanding times.

For churches to offer testimony to God in our society now, we shall need to be unembarrassed about the unpredictable and passionate God of Scripture. We shall need to connect with the long tradition of wisdom and celebrate worship, blessing, abundance, difference held in friendship, cries of agony and desire and the utter love of the Trinity. To be formed in the image of the Trinity is to participate in that same movement of Jesus towards the Father and so towards the whole of Creation. The Church is meant to be the joyful place where we know God's delight in us and where we can be transformed.

It is urgent, therefore, that we have confidence to go beyond the present institutional dilemmas. We may be roused from apathy, complacency or even a death wish when we become alert to the ways God never stops coming towards us in people, texts, situations and communities, luring us into newness of understanding and life. We know how to be a Good Friday people and increasingly a Holy Saturday people, but what about Easter Day and Pentecost? Instead of seeing the Holy Spirit as the impressive or terrifying prerogative of Pentecostals, all churches must become schools of learning in the Spirit. Christian faith is not a following of carefully prescribed instructions but praying in the Spirit (Ephesians 6.18), worship in the Spirit (Philippians 3.3), discerning the Spirit (1 Corinthians 2.15).

5

Formed in the walking of Jesus

Community formed in encountering and being healed by Jesus

A pilgrimage is a kind of wandering, open to the contingencies of space and time, which is at the same time a gradual discovery of purpose. Through a life of pilgrimage, one acquires knowledge of God's purposes, and one discovers that a pilgrim's life is measured by these purposes. To walk in the paths of God is to have one's steps measured by God. This means we are measured by an infinite measure: our paths are not therefore fixed in any way we can imagine, nor do we live in a fixed universe.

(Daniel W. Hardy 2010, p. 59)

Incarnation, cross, resurrection

Restlessness, hope, dissatisfaction and an intense desire that people will know God's love and forgiveness and will choose to be agents of God's kingdom lie at the heart of becoming Church. It's a work in progress, personal and communal. Developing a moving, pilgrim or walking understanding of Church makes a connection with the fragmented and shifting nature of contemporary living. Critically it demonstrates in the present Jesus doing the Father's transformative work through the Spirit in bodily practices. In what follows I am using 'walking' as a metaphor for Church created by both Jesus Christ and the Spirit, as a transfiguring interruption to stability, expecting the wonder of God's new possibilities. Many of the examples I list below are familiar signs of the reformulation of Church in our day.

Five active dimensions can be identified in a 'moving ecclesiology':

- promoting healing;
- moving in response to circumstances;
- always changing;
- celebrating difference;
- connecting with others beyond itself.

We see this, for example, in Jesus' walking the lanes of Galilee among a varied group of disciples: healing, challenging, reinstating, drawing into the kingdom, comforting and awakening response. The narrative of a pilgrim Church includes Jesus' exchange with those being crucified with him (Luke 23.39–43) and the Emmaus story (Luke 24.13–35). The Church's inspiration is Jesus walking with groups and communities, interacting, opening up their minds through being present sacramentally, not as an idea but as present fellow traveller and conversation partner.

Ignatian spirituality, evolving from the sixteenth-century conversion experience and leadership of Ignatius of Loyola (see <www.isc-glasgow.co.uk>), brings together many of the strands of the Church's renewal. This Christian pathway invites us to a life of transformation through entering into the sounds, smells, pictures, impact, affirmation and disquiet of Gospel narratives. Through the accounts of Jesus' birth, charismatic healing ministry, praying, appearing in court, being flogged and crucified, and bursting into the lives of disciples with unknown newness, we can re-imagine Church as a purposeful response. Through the intensity of the reality of God in Jesus, a space opens where, as Church and as persons, we are invited to a liberating journey.

The concept of Church on the move leads to virtues and practices of knowing Jesus Christ in the poor and humiliated and in the joyful and exuberant, including ourselves. In its deepest form the Eucharist draws out in us a core commitment of receiving and giving love, and the community of the Church. Constantly returning to the core centre of faith that is Jesus of Nazareth crucially draws out the identity of the Eucharistic community. Dynamic ways of celebrating the Eucharist as advance sign of the final transformation of the world sends the Church to find people in the remotest, saddest, most distorted, starving, diseased and conflicted spaces, including our own lives (Matthew 25.35). To become Church measured by the walking of Jesus is part of God's call to all humanity, to 'Go inside. Start any-where. Follow it everywhere' (see page 53).

The Gospel writers tell us very little of the conditions of the walking mission of Jesus, except that a group of women provided for their needs (Luke 8.3) and 'the Son of Man has nowhere to lay his head' (Luke 9.58). Imagine the moving camp as a pointer to Church, with people being associated with it and participating in a variety of ways, those in dire need seeking it out in cries of distress, with Jesus discerning where to go next and sending disciples on to prepare the way.

To become Church on the pattern of that travelling mission means, in whatever circumstances, living in praise and joy, welcome and abundance. A landlord in a Herefordshire village invited the parish church to lead a service in his pub. It went well, as leaflets were dished out and many took part. The suggestion, 'Why don't we open up the Church and do this kind of thing more often?' was countered by the riposte 'No, God is here, behind the bar.' The attractive image of God was one of warmth, welcome and closeness.

The practices of community and priest in a walking ecclesiology might be:

- *Promoting healing* through a monthly healing service, critically inclusive of a variety of forms of music; at the celebration of St Luke each year shaping the Sunday Eucharist around the healing ministry; including preaching, prayer and laying on of hands frequently at or in association with regular services; purposefully including all our personal brokenness in the life of the community; finding ways of challenging disruptive or un-Christian behaviour; helping people, through receiving acceptance, to stop identifying themselves only from the place where they are wounded. This is Christian community in action and it can be demanding for those taking a lead to be always inviting the congregation to see a bigger picture through greater intimacy with God.

- An example of *moving in response to circumstances* would be the redevelopment of the musical life of a congregation when the inherited pattern is no longer in tune with the worshipping life as a whole. One parish came very late to the idea of a nave altar. With the advantage of having chairs in the nave rather than pews, gradually, through experimenting for special occasions, they agreed that a nave altar table would be the centre of Sunday worship. This left a robed choir sitting isolated in the chancel. It was also the case that the singers no longer had strong voices and the congregation had little confidence in its own voice. With the support of the thinking and writing and personal encouragement of Richard Giles, some now centre music energy in a voluntary music coordinator. Instead of the robed choir they have developed a group of singers of all ages who sit distinctly but close to the congregation. Such an arrangement feeds the overall vision of worship that is participative and further creates a relational understanding of God, worship and Church. A parish priest offers an example of when a parish moved spontaneously to move an east-facing altar. She describes how this evolved unexpectedly through being in discussion with flower arrangers in the sanctuary prior to Harvest, her first in the parish. A new surge of willingness to be involved in the decorating naturally embraced and took forward this change. It never came to the PCC, nor had she even reached the stage when she would broach the subject. It was a matter of 'groundswell'.

- To be *always changing* might seem very irritating to some personality types. But an obvious example in some clusters of parishes and deaneries is alertness to ensuring that Mission Action Planning and the task groups that deliver against it are reviewed regularly. Local ministry development teams, in all shapes and sizes, are reviewing progress, encouraging, asking searching questions, making connections between various ministry and mission initiatives. These are illustrations of a walking ecclesiology as opposed to a static, given, passivity-creating way of Church. Meeting Jesus and walking with him is to know that nothing, not even the best plans of yesterday, can remain still because the Holy Spirit is co-creator of Church and lovingly breeds the dissatisfaction and restlessness that leads to innovation and increased desire to serve God's kingdom.

- *Celebrating difference* can be illustrated from the variety of ways that deaneries and parishes are promoting learning:
  - in year-round small groups with relatively stable membership;
  - through Justice and Peace groups;
  - through the Mothers' Union or men's group;
  - in occasional or seasonal groups as a primary way of building discipleship;

- as an adult learning process leading to baptism or confirmation but including other members of the Church;
- in Advent evening worship devised and presented by groups of laity.

One priest writes of the learning in her situation,

> If you took someone walking through the door in September and they have got quietly involved, they would then be invited to join 'The Shock of the New' which is 'here's what we do and here's what church is' in straightforward terms. They would then be encouraged very gently to become part of the worshipping life of the church by engagement with, say, an evening service where they might read from Scripture. Once they had built a pattern of worshipping life someone might invite them to join a Lent group or perhaps give it a break and then after Easter when the Confirmation Group begins, they say 'Would you like to join a confirmation group?'
>
> That would take them through to November and then having taken part in a worship service, they might be asked if they were interested in using their skills in presenting a series of Advent Services. Then they might want to do an overt, more directed piece of discipleship learning in, say, a Lent group. So someone in an eighteen-month time frame could have passed through several ways of engaging and met different groups of people and engaged a range of ways of thinking and different parts of their whole person in doing that.

This narrative is one way of demonstrating what a Trinitarian ecclesiology could be like in practice. First, engagement with worship at ever deeper levels of involvement over time is seen as central to formation of newcomers into the life of the church. Second, the idea of progression through a series of small sub-groups of the community captures the notion that building a wide set of relationships in the congregation will develop the quality of community as well as integrate the newcomers. It expresses and extends the idea of *communion*, and its links both to learning and worship reinforce for newcomers a corporate spiritual identity. Third, the engagement with 'different parts of the person' reflects a high degree of commitment in this church community to a sophisticated understanding of adult learning. (I am grateful for the insights here of the Receptive Ecumenism process and in particular to Helen Savage.) Christian communities that learn corporately and individually to help others to know how to become disciples in their own unique way have learnt the art of walking with new disciples that with Jesus was a blend of profound respect and urgent challenge.

- *Connecting with others beyond ourselves* happens in many places largely through the daily lives of the congregation with neighbours and family, in schools and colleges, in business, medical practice, government departments, Rotary, golf club, ecumenical projects such as WaterAid, Christian Aid, food banks and Street Pastors. The shopping centre connection (page 138) would be a particular example to note.

A relational way of being Church is always open to what the Spirit is now suggesting. It is messy, contingent and knows its areas of weakness. Rather than hiding from such brokenness, a gracious Church will choose to recognize that all the green lights will never be lit simultaneously. Thankful for all that can be assessed as creative and formative, our task is to find the resilience to continue developing excellence in our practice. What seems central is for churches to give priority to adult formation in faith and spirituality in which ordained and licensed ministers are facilitators and part of the creation of a learning ethos.

Led by the Spirit

After Pentecost, Jesus Christ and the Holy Spirit are decisively at the heart of the continuing tradition whose early years are narrated by Luke in Acts. One striking feature of that story is the daring innovation that it is possible to go beyond any precedents in the lifetime of Jesus. This is not a conception of tradition as continuing to repeat literally the sorts of things Jesus did. The most striking example is the decision to open the gospel to Gentiles (the baptism of Cornelius, Acts 10 and 11, and the decision of the Council of Jerusalem articulated by James in Acts 15).

The Holy Spirit has brought about a radical innovation within the Christian tradition that opens up the possibility of Church in practices of mutuality, reciprocity, friendship and generous exchange. The reappraisal of Trinitarian doctrine over the past half-century has moved thinking, and to some degree practice, from inherited linear and stepped-down hierarchical assumptions.

Fed by centuries of worship, meditation and rigorous debate, the Trinitarian understanding of God is the most concentrated distillation of Christian wisdom. This identification of God arises within the narratives of Jesus' baptism and resurrection, Pentecost, Paul's account of Christian prayer in Romans 8 and the Farewell Discourses of John (chapters 13–17). In washing the feet of the disciples, the Son of God, Lord and Master, reveals a deeper divine authority exercised through humility, service and love, through a communion of hearts in closeness, friendliness, openness and humility, bridging the gap between those over and those under their leadership.

To know and respond to the life of the Trinity is to experience and be embraced by difference, otherness and multiplicity in God. While some Christians believe the doctrine of the Trinity to be a mistake, other contemplative–theological reflections of recent times have variously conceived of the Holy Spirit as the completer and communicator of the work of Christ, as the uniting bond between Father and Son, as prototype of persons in relationship or as the means of incorporation into the Trinitarian life of God.

This last, incorporative type arises from reflection on Romans 8.9–30, Paul's description of the wisdom of the prayer of the Risen Christ. It is in praying that the disciple is drawn into the knowledge of God as irreducibly three. Here the Spirit is not just continuing in time the revelation of Christ or enabling disciples to recognize him, but is drawing the ones who pray into the life of God (as redeemed daughters and sons, as Paul says). There are clear connections here with Luke's account of Jesus' baptism and his theology of the Spirit creating the Church in the Acts of the Apostles as well as in the experience of prayer, worship and especially the Eucharist.

The doctrine of the Trinity must be used in an analogous and not mechanical way. It sometimes seems as though the doctrine is seized upon, unsubtly, in support of particular notions of relating. But given the way that the Holy Spirit is unpredictably and continually leading the Church into new truth, we must be alert to dangers of becoming permanently fixated upon one way of speaking of the Trinity. In a wisdom tradition we can enjoy the huge variety of available biblical and allegorical allusions, poetic imagination and narrative as well as prose, constantly reread in new situations, protecting us from complacency and too rigid forms of expression.

Anglican priest and academic Malcolm Guite (2012) shows how when we step inside poetry and allow ourselves to be formed by it we make deeper connections with the way things are, and so connect with God. He reminds us how Christian poetry through every century can take us surely into the Trinitarian pattern of interconnection, as Creation shares in the divine life. Guite's proposal that 'This cleansing and training of vision through a revitalized imagination is a common task for science, poetry and theology' (2012, p. 244) opens a way of living with complexity in faith at the same time as being open to its transforming power.

In the following chapter we shall ask what practices and virtues will be required in a Spirit-led Church.

6

From strategies to virtues

Choosing and living practices to build the Church's
character and purpose

The whole world is shook up, so what are you going to do when
things fall apart? You're either going to become more fundamentalist and try to hold things together, or you're going to
forsake the old ambitions and goals and live life as an experiment, making it up as you go along.

(Pema Chödrön in Wheatley and Frieze 2011, Preface)

A virtue ecclesiology

In terms of sharing in God's mission, the word 'strategy' seems a
very thin diet. In this chapter we shall explore how Church both as
institution and as local community has the urgent task of carrying
in its practices the deepest meaning of Church. Also, instead of a
dichotomy between Church as a reality created by the Holy Sprit and
as a human organization, we will explore how the two together can
witness to the new order begun in the resurrection of Jesus Christ
and a foretaste of God's ultimate desire for Creation. Such a way of
Church will be able to accept the realities of and learn from all who
suffer and are marginalized as well as to bear the apathy of an atheist
and individualist culture.

In every situation, churches make choices about how far they
define themselves as naturally embroiled in culture or as world-
renouncing. Although churches define themselves as communities
of the baptized drawn towards God and God's final purposes, the
canvas for the Church's work is the whole of God's Trinitarian work
within the whole of the world. Paul indicates a virtuous vision for
Church rooted in love that includes God's life in the whole of life, so

avoiding a polarizing approach: 'And now faith, hope and love abide, these three; and the greatest of these is love' (1 Corinthians 13.13).

The concept of virtue ecclesiology, adapted from the work of Alasdair MacIntyre, notably by Gerard Mannion and Geoff Moore, provides a framework helpful to this exploration. Rather than a blueprint, universally applicable, Mannion advocates an ecclesiology 'from below' that will 'aid the concrete church in performing its task of witness and pastoral care' (Mannion 2007, p. 37). His proposal is for a virtue- or character-orientated way of Church focused primarily on the goal it wishes to reach.

MacIntyre's theories of virtue

MacIntyre advances the notion of practice–institution combinations. His work leads to the question of how individuals might place themselves in communal settings that seek an overall purpose, rather than focusing on rules, principles or outcomes for individual happiness. MacIntyre emphasizes the enduring nature for institutions of 'virtues' over theories, paradigms, models or strategies. He describes how 'practices' build up individuals and cooperative activity in desired 'virtues' that serve the agreed long-term goals of an organization, emphasizing the priority of love. He writes:

> [The virtues are] those dispositions which will not only sustain practices and enable us to achieve the goals internal to practices, but which will also sustain us in the relevant kind of quest for the good, by enabling us to overcome the harms, dangers and temptations and distractions which we encounter, and which will furnish us with increasing self-knowledge and increasing knowledge of the good. (MacIntyre 2007, p. 219).

Geoff Moore of the Durham University Business School has accumulated a body of empirical work that draws on this approach. Although the application has mainly been to business organizations, more loosely aligned church institutions and their practices of faith can also find helpful connections. To explore the possibilities of MacIntyre's work on organizations for churches, understanding his definition of a 'practice' is essential.

In MacIntyre's theory:

- Practice involves engagement in social activity.
- Practice leads to 'internal goods', such as excellence without limit, for all concerned, in both performance and performer. By contrast, 'external goods' created by practices (say, reputation or profit) are always in short supply and to be competed for.
- Assessment of the quality of a practice is always in relation to predecessors in the performance of the practice (perhaps playing an instrument) and especially those who have reached through to new levels of excellence. So a contemporary performer is both encouraged and challenged by the tradition in which he or she stands.
- Practices have not only a history but a future yet to be reached, and one that will be the constant subject of debate among present practitioners.

What MacIntyre calls 'internal goods' are available only to participants and can be tested only by performers. For example, the television commentator has a limited understanding of the satisfaction, combining pain, discipline, skill and desire, that is required in a cross-channel swimmer or an Olympic gold medallist.

Church virtues and practices

Our concern here is to investigate how Church can healthily develop to meet new circumstances. The relationship between local church practice and the practice of Church as institution is important to consider. Our experience is often of frustration that the institution – 'the Diocese', 'they' – doesn't understand or care and seems not to be working to the same agenda as the parishes. Yet in reality, no bishop or diocese would disclaim an interest in working towards high achievement in its performance of its practices.

Church activity always comes culturally freighted. All practices are formed not only in the life of the Risen Christ and the energy of the Spirit, but within specific environments and in the power dynamics of organizations. In MacIntyre's terms, there is routinely tension between the internal and external goods of a church both locally and as institution. Therefore, to keep internal and external goods in balance, a diocese, as institution, will need to strive to have

healthy finances, property in serviceable condition, an ethical investment policy, a pension fund for central staff and a sense of their being
appreciated. But problems arise when that seems to be the limit of its
aspirations.

What MacIntyre proposes concerning institutional virtues links
creatively with the notion of a wisdom tradition way of Church. A
parish, or cluster of parishes, deanery or diocese could decide to
aspire to virtues chosen to serve its stated goal. In cooperation with
other churches, it might adopt and constantly revise practices – with
both internal and external outcomes – most likely to promote the
exercise of the virtues required to achieve its ultimate shared sense of
purpose. This might be, for example, to give a secure and resourceful
environment for local churches to flourish.

The point MacIntyre makes is that however significant or influential a particular worker may come to be within the organization, it
is vital that no one ever thinks he or she can fulfil that role without
striving to live the communal virtues and seeking excellence in agreed
core practices. At any point in its organization, it is vital that the dis-
tinguishing practices that serve the virtues and goal of a church be in
evidence. So a bishop will learn to know intuitively when a pastoral
visit is suddenly priority over some other part of his work or an archdeacon will know when to postpone a meeting to meet an emergency.

MacIntyre notes how easy it is for there to be a conflict when external goods (finance, buildings and human resource levels) are allowed
to take priority over internal goods (in the Church's case, pastoral
care, sacramental celebration or contextual engagement with Scripture). The task of clergy and lay leaders is always to watch out for a
balance between the search for excellence between internal and external goods and certainly to notice when one is flourishing to the detriment of the other. The corporate search for and communication of a
good ultimate purpose for the Church is clearly vital if the virtues and
practices are to be upheld in every part of the texture of the institution and at every point of contact with the population. It would make
no sense, for example, for the administration of a cathedral car park
to be operating through practices that were in sharp contrast to the
espoused virtues of the cathedral church in its sacramental functions.

The corporate search for and communication of a good ultimate purpose for a diocese or province is clearly vital if its virtues
and practices are to be upheld in every part of the texture of the

institution and at every point of contact with the population. Perhaps the gift to society of a complex and loosely ordered institution like the Church of England is precisely the virtue of excellence in the matching of its internal and external practices, in preaching and portfolio investment.

There will naturally be dispute concerning the ultimate purpose of the Church, depending on the weight given to differing understandings of God or to texts and narratives of Scripture. When it comes to identifying core practices that sustain the Church in its virtues and ultimate purpose, some would emphasize the Church's pastoral aspect, while others might prefer to speak of building up the community of God's people through the development of spiritual gifts. Others might choose worship, witness, justice and peace, growth in discipleship, prophetic engagement with society or the celebration of the Eucharist.

Moore is especially appreciative of Samuel Wells' framework of practices, which he adapts, recognizing that Wells is not using language exactly as MacIntyre does. Here is a distillation of Wells' (2006) generic practices for churches, together with related activities:

- *forming* through evangelism, catechesis
- *incorporating* through baptism
- *performing* through praying, sharing life, faith and troubles together in the body of Christ, welcoming the stranger
- *restoring* through speaking the truth, repentance, forgiveness, reconciliation, restoration, healing
- *Eucharist* through practices of meeting, hearing, responding, sharing, going.

Apparently genial – but in fact manipulative – hierarchical forms of power breed powerlessness and a culture of infantilizing and competitiveness. In all disciplines and professions the resistance towards, and desire for, strong leadership continues to be a contentious issue. Tim Greenwood, Co-Director/Psychologist of Living Systems Ltd, describes inviting a group of staff in a school to consider 'the radical middle', by which he means a balance between adult-led and child-led questions and between questions that activate ideas and those that contain a suggested course of action. What emerged was deep ambivalence in some of the more long-standing members of the team to moving away from polarized forms of practice because a relational – 'present' – way of teaching seemed too far from their current practice. He comments that it would have needed a shift in paradigm, a move away from fatalism to daring to hope for real contact in the classroom! Those of us who lead in churches can probably own a similar ambivalence.

Experience teaches that supposedly 'strong' or 'clear' leadership often leaves others powerless. It's also true that context must be an influence on the style of leadership to be adopted, but we tend to resist rather than follow with our whole selves when things are forced upon us. None of us acts responsibly on behalf of plans and programmes created without us. Our resistance is to being the *object* of change rather than the *agent* of change. Such methods destroy the very energy needed to learn and imagine and contribute to the future. Processes of mutual discovery, creativity and scaling across that include the hearts and minds of everyone concerned generate satisfaction and commitment.

Illustrations of church virtues

A renewed culture of being present, listening to local initiatives, welcoming diversity, sharing ideas and resources generously and scaling across needs to be more than an aberration from the certainties of the past. It must be rooted in the expectation of healing and innovation and boldly explored in its practices.

Virtues for MacIntyre lie behind practices. They are the traits of character in an organization that make a variety of practices possible and over time help an institution move towards its purpose. For several years the final purpose of the church where I serve as parish priest has been expressed as 'Making Christ known through building his Church'. Over time, a variety of virtues and practices have been pursued to hold the church in this identifying purpose.

Three of the virtues that have grown in this church and that I believe to be very significant for the wise flourishing of any intentional performance of the gospel in our culture are those of celebrating abundance, difference and uncertainty. Earlier I placed great emphasis on listening and being in a place, and not just observing it from the outside. I offer what follows in the spirit of 'scaling across'. If this is a virtue for us, in our situation, what would be a virtue for you?

Living in a spirit of abundance

Jesus shows us God's superabundance, from the sign of the wedding at Cana (John 2), through sharing meals and companionship with people, and in his rising from death when Creation is restored and his disciples are led to worship, to be his friends and eat with him (Wells 2006). Scripture is full of invitations to accept hope or live with despair, to choose whether or not to live with an attitude of scarcity or of abundance, the way of Pharaoh or the way of the Lord. If our true desire is to follow Jesus and to be the Risen Christ, there's no room for pathos or self-pity about the present profile of religious practice.

In and between churches we need vision, determination, knowledge and the experience to help our churches navigate this particular time. Jesus showed us the way in turning water into excellent wine and the feeding with the loaves and fish. It's about abundance in community. We can't go it alone. It's time to network and be connected as a basic way of being. If we think we have a shortage we're looking in the wrong place. All that we need is here.

Energy and joy will be rediscovered when we go into and remain still in that deep place where we know God's presence. We live in a time when so many public institutions are short of cash and human resources. What an achievement it would be if weary institutional churches that are short of the traditional resources on which they previously relied could, in the trauma of radical change, be known for their outrageously joyful sense of abundance.

Celebrating difference

Our quest is for churches to model immediacy, face-to-face presence and reciprocity as advance signs of a human society free of injustice and oppression. Communion requires being-in-openness (freedom), being-in-transcendence (ecstasy) and being ourselves (a relational network of communion).

Our task is to liberate, to release, to help local churches recognize, celebrate and cooperate with all the narratives, experiences, talents and gifts being offered to us. Paulo Freire, the South American educator, strove to get people to recognize their complementary gifts and to harness them together. In *Pedagogy of the Oppressed*, he wrote 'Leaders who do not act dialogically, but insist on imposing their decisions, do not organize the people – they manipulate them. They do not liberate, nor are they liberated: they oppress' (Freire 2000, p. 127).

Embracing uncertainty

The Church doesn't need our false selves, ego trips, grand designs or heroic ministers who are always right and always available. Gustavo Gutierrez, the liberation theologian, when asked if he ever had doubts about his way of doing Church, replied, 'Every morning.'

A question for all with responsibility today is, 'Do I have the courage to be a disappointment to many and to myself in order to do what only I am called to within the virtuous circle of the churches in which I have a role?' In a society that reacts against faith by believing in nothing, there's a temptation for churches to lust for absolute certainty. There's a myth that possessing unsinkable truths, fixed boundaries and unquestioned belief are sure signs of a strong community. Church experience, for example, in Latin American Pentecostalism is summarized by Ivone Gebara:

> Religions of instant salvation are growing; they offer miraculous cures, promise jobs, do exorcisms, appear to give people an identity, and generate moments of shared euphoria. But even as these religions play into the hands of the established system, they seem not to see the logic of destruction that is growing visibly in our economically globalized society.
>
> (Gebara 1999, p. 198)

Part of this seduction is the visible evidence that strong churches, simplifying complexity, have an accelerated growth rate. But our concern here is to learn from the wisdom tradition how little security is needed when we worship God for God's sake and love Creation as God loves. The Gospels speak of the disruptive and surprising acts of God in Incarnation and resurrection. They are full of events where disciples, steeped in tradition, are surprised and afraid at so much that is innovative. The early centuries were peppered with sharp debates and struggles about faith in Christ.

Anglicans have a long tradition of commitment to the interweaving of the life of God within the complexities of society and Creation.

A pilgrim people looks for truth by simultaneously diving deep into God and into reality. Theologians such as Karl Barth have explored authentic simplicity as lying within the fullness of an abundant God. The writer of Ephesians speaks of the 'mystery' of the gospel (Ephesians 6.19).

We are considering the practice of faith – rather than grand theories – in terms of sustaining local Christian presence in particular places that are linked to one another. Churches find it hard to know by what criterion we could reach agreement on important issues – not solely Scripture, tradition, reason or practice. So staying connected and in conversation and letting truth blossom and grow locally and regionally in courtesy is a key ecclesial virtue.

There is so much in Christian history and tradition and in Jewish Scripture to reinforce this. Churches are not resident aliens but drawn to heaven while rooted in earth. We stand at crossroads, on boundaries, at in-between places with an in-between God, at a place that resonates with field theories where events take place on the divisions between people, with quantum physics, and with Foucault's theories of dynamic power in local networks. Navigating and enjoying complexity in a changing world requires our willingness to keep learning to think differently, to work in relationships and teams, to be intentionally part of a community, to expect chaos to be the normal route to creativity, change and growth.

An obituary of a jazz percussionist described his playing as combining intensity with restraint.

> [He used to say,] 'Listen closely, take a chance, keep going even if money's tight and you'll feel the real reward.' He didn't need to play loud or be loud to get that intensity. It's like splitting diamonds. If you know exactly the right place to make the impact, you don't need to hit anything hard.   (*Guardian* 2012)

Malcolm Guite (2012), exploring the poetry of Seamus Heaney, George Herbert, Philip Larkin and T. S. Eliot, invites us to be ready to hear more than one voice and to delight in ambiguity:

> Words are not dry little counters, each betokening one meaning. Even the smallest and driest of words is like the small dry seeds that fall through Heaney's 'Rain Stick', suddenly evoking

through their music all the refreshing downpour he celebrates. We have to let the words *be* music, and in that music to let them play counter-melodies to one another.   (Guite 2012, p. 27)

Christian power chooses the way of intimacy and vulnerability rather than domination or the oversimplification of complexity. It is shown in Jesus' walking through Galilee, all the way to the cross, preached and lived as healing, humility, love, mutual service, friendship, courtesy and hospitality. Christ asks his followers to be on the move in this same way for the promotion of healing in every part of life and sends the Spirit to make it possible. After Easter the disciples had more confidence that, despite everything, they were forgiven, and felt more assured of a place within the Father's purposes. But it was only at Pentecost that their diffidence turned into an exuberance easily confused with joyful inebriation.

The desire for trustworthy paths is understandable, but as in the psalms and the pictures we have of the walking of Jesus' disciples and apostles, being uncertain about God, being confronted with God's hiddenness, is part of the very nature and possibility of having faith in real life. We come to it and lose it and find it again at different moments in our pilgrimage. Doubt, uncertainty and disagreement are not accidental, unusual features of religious experience but actually make it what it is.

Keeping Church true to its virtues in conflict

As described earlier, my own recent experience includes leading a community in which a vocal minority were resistant to changing the internal layout of the church building, though with hindsight there is a recognition that much of the proposed works were simply delayed housekeeping (heating, lighting, replastering, painting, upgrading the parish office and toilets and providing a kitchen). As parish priest I found myself constantly having to hold the boundary between this local church and the wider Church and between various groups who were not listening to one another. I had also to balance my own impatience with those who seemed to be wanting to be locked in the past with the need to hold the community to its identity through public conversations that didn't diminish or scapegoat others.

The need for change and possible ways forward had been on the agenda long before my arrival as vicar. The staff team continued to help the community reflect, in learning and preaching, on the need to have a building that helped us, more than the current layout was able, to speak of God as among us as well as transcendent. In conversation and experimental liturgy we explored other important aspects of and metaphors for the Trinitarian God. Although the Holy Mystery we call 'God' exposes the limits of human speech, the language we favour in our generation for relationships, such as nurturing, caring, embracing, mothering, sustaining, respecting, compassion, anguish, freedom, personhood, tenderness and love, conveys many of our experiences of God.

In the public hearing of the Consistory Court that eventually ensued, I explained the church council's rationale. There was a strong desire among us to provide a space for liturgy that could give access to God's holy and friendly presence among us in life's difficulties and in building inclusive community. A key element of our mission was to be a church identified through friendship, inspiring worship, growth in the Spirit of God, creating a real sense of belonging, gift-based ministries, developing a vision and effective structures, growing leaders and evangelizing that is responsive to need.

In other words, to share in the mission of God in the whole of life and to draw all people closer to God were our primary objectives. Our desired modification of the building was a practical expression of this. We delighted in school visits, art college exhibitions, concerts, drama and social events already accommodated in the rich and open space given to us by the original architects.

We recognized that over previous decades many churches had created nave sanctuaries. Experience showed that many of the earlier examples suffered through being too small, temporary-looking and apologetic. In its present form the dominant note of St Mary's is of God's distance, majesty and separateness. From its inception, Sunday worship encompassed the entire length of the building. The purpose of confidently placing a round, solid, central sanctuary between the ambos will say that, for the coming decades, at least – and who knows where future generations will make their contribution – rather than focusing on a liturgy offered by a chosen few (clergy, servers and choristers within the apse and chancel) to be observed by the laity in general, we intended to become a 'round' community of people of varying temperaments. Being open to the neighbourhood yet strengthened by gathering around the altar is the keystone of our identity as God's people.

I emphasized how our proposals were rooted in a scriptural and pilgrim theology that says, 'Whatever God and God's people may have done yesterday, what is happening today is of most significance for us.' We saw no evidence in the history of church architecture to support the view that new generations must act timidly, so that 'wiser' people coming later can 'revert' to what everyone accepts as a 'norm'. A key element in re-ordering the church in the twenty-first century was to recognize that our common life is fostered by new and evolving learning and worship styles. Being 'present' to God, to one another and to the world would be strengthened by creating a new dynamic between the two main worship spaces (the nave and the chancel).

Further, the new sanctuary, at the same level as the chancel floor, would offer greater visibility to the whole congregation. It would also be a theological statement about us becoming more a community constituted in collaboration, inclusion and equality, as a rebalancing of a previous overemphasis on clergy dependence and linear hierarchy.

The church council was motivated by a desire to hold in creative tension both the wonder and the intimacy associated with the Trinitarian God, rather than the inherited overemphasis on transcendence and distance. Worship in recent times has increasingly reminded us that there are many ways in which we can sit and stand together in worship that hold a wide range of moods and experiences.

Allowing for great flexibility, our need was for a worship space in the nave that allowed us to experience and learn more of the God who comes close, as well as who holds together the life of the universe. 'Sharing' the sacrament of Holy Communion with one another, in mutuality, standing, was an experience that many had come to recognize as a profound statement of how we come to know God, not in the abstract but in the open relationship with our neighbours and fellow pilgrims of every age.

The opening up of the previous choir stall space would allow for a quiet reflective area in the present chancel area for smaller midweek services, groups and gatherings of many kinds. A new moveable but substantial table altar, placed on a dais west of the chancel, could be used in either direction as required or temporarily removed for a concert or drama.

To create, as the fulcrum of the building, a sensitive, clean, crisp circle would be a reminder of the inclusive circle of disciples who gathered around Jesus and his prophetic, healing work (Luke 9). It is also contemporary, positive and confident in what it says about our relationship with God and each other. The Chancellor took his time in finding for the church council and many people contributed to the main agenda of holding the community together while insisting that we re-create the worship space to serve God's mission as we best understand it now.

This example of a network of influences that had to be held ultimately by the incumbent (with colleagues and the council) illustrates how the practices of decision-making need to be of a piece with what is to be decided. And it is costly and demanding work that cannot be hurried. My own learning through this is that the process should probably have taken even longer and involved more conversation. Also, the priest has to hold the pain of being the bridge between one church and the whole Church. In a catholic ordering, clergy and lay leaders sometimes have to be bold and determined and take risks for the growth in wisdom of the whole community. I could not have held to this without the networks of family, staff, council, diocese, personal work supervision and the skill, previous experience and character of one individual, named by the Chancellor who ruled in favour of the council's vision for a building that would help us to learn more of God's inclusive relationality.

Virtues, according to MacIntyre, are long-term characteristics of an organization that are visible in and measured by all their practices. As Moore summarizes neatly:

> the possession and exercise of the virtues enables an individual (in community with other practitioners of course) to achieve the goods internal to the practice, and the achievement of those goods *across a variety of practices and over time* is instrumental in the individual's search for and movement towards their own *telos* or purpose.　　　　　　　　(Moore 2012, p. 51)

Parishes that continually engage with the processes of Mission Action Planning learn about congregational consultation and communication to identify their final purpose, and therefore virtues and practices. Dioceses, through promoting, nurturing and listening attentively to active networking rather than announcing centralized policies or laissez-faire approaches, considerably enhance this process.

7

Grown-up Church

Maturing through personal and corporate awareness

What priests do is to secure the opportunity for the priestly people to announce who they are – to themselves but also to the world around: they are trustees of the time and space for worship that can be characterized as the action of the whole of the believing community . . . so that society around can see that it is still indestructibly and non-negotiably there.

(Rowan Williams in Wells and Coakley 2008, p. 180)

Spiritual maturity for sustaining creative change

Rowan Williams describes the priestly role as re-presenting to the whole Church in the liturgy its identity as the believing community of God's people. Although the underlying assumption of this whole book is that the entire people of God is invited to participate from their Spirit-gifts to the present and future Church, our persistent dependency on clergy means that the self-awareness of priests and bishops is of intense significance.

Priests presiding in local churches need a deep conviction of the Church's true nature as community as well as a personal security to give others freedom to be creative. The Church's history and polity means that the influence of the priest is inevitably instrumental, and the long-term lack of serious development of lay learning and spirituality leaves a heavy deficit.

An inexorably diminishing number of stipendiary clergy clearly cannot and should not be trying to fill every ministry space as perceived in the old pattern. Yet every priest brings different skills and priorities and every parochial situation is unique. To act *as if* churches are already being reinvigorated through a recognition that everyone's contribution counts is the change we want to see. Living in the moment, being present, is to practise believing in the transforming power of God's love working through virtues and habits that enrich the entire Church in its life and witness.

Dioceses that commit to the expectation that, in different ways, all with a lively faith will participate in being Church, will abandon the notion that the paid priest is the automatic or chief 'carrier' of the rich meaning of the gospel. They can let go of the lingering anxiety that ideally each parish should have a stipendiary priest. Fundamentally this demands a reappraisal and recognition of the place of all God's people in building up churches in life and a desire that others are drawn towards God through the life of Christian community.

In patches, this is happening already, especially in rural areas where the mission and liturgy of multiple parishes is held in a loose unity of oversight by *episkope* priests. An internet search for 'multiple parish benefices' reveals the extent of the urgent conversations around this sharp topic, such as the Pastoral Organization section of the Diocese of Salisbury website (<www.salisbury.anglican.org/parishes/organisat ion/?searchterm=pastoral%20organisation>). The website of the 5+ Rural Learning Network for Multi-Parish Benefice Clergy (<www. arthurrankcentre.org.uk/library-of-good-practice/item/6677-5%20 -rural-learning-network-for-multi-parish-benefice-clergy>) opens the door on a great deal of hidden anxiety in the Church, as exemplified by 'It's good to talk – but you don't really understand my situation.' Conversations with many in 'front-line' parochial ministry indicate that this is a not uncommon yet largely unspoken feeling:

> It can seem harder to find others who truly understand, let alone empathise with not just the struggles and disappointments but with what really are the achievements and encouragements in that setting. Plenty will listen, many will sympathise, some will try to understand but far fewer will succeed. To be fair, before you can understand you may have had to 'be there'; live it, breathe it, have felt the pulse of a place and its people. But that's not likely to happen, is it? Or is it? (Brian Pearson 2012)

The Rural Learning Network is seen by participants as an antidote to isolationism. Convenor and facilitator Steve Annandale (from the

Diocese of Bath and Wells School of Formation) admits that he sees members leaving a session with as many questions – possibly more – than when they arrived, but that is not the point. He says,

> The genius of the group is that others *recognise* the questions. Some have been able to 're-frame' them so they have become manageable – even solvable. This is a group that does not set out to deliver solutions but it does offer clarification and insight only feasible through shared experience.

Pearson continues:

> The phrase 'I know where you are coming from' has never been so apt. What is shared has the authentic ring of credibility – a refreshing change from some generalized 'worthy words' that have little hope of being transformed into anything that can be applied back at the 'pew-face' in deepest rural Somerset.
>
> One beneficiary and 'fan' of the Rural Learning Network is Andrew Chalkley, Rector of Beckington with Standerwick, Berkley, Rodden, Lullington with Orchardleigh. Andrew says, 'Rural ministry demands that church leaders both prop up Christendom and act as apostolic missionaries, and so anything that helps towards a "big picture" strategy is most welcome.'
>
> (Pearson 2012)

The internet has many other examples of clergy asking questions together and being a resource for one another (for example through Skype conversations). I also know, from conversations, of other clergy who cannot find time for such networking because it would mean a complete restructuring of the way in which they are working. It seems vital that other lay and ordained ministers and wardens should have opportunity for such mutual support beyond the business of deanery synods.

Where the stipendiary priest has sufficient encouragement from the bishop and the diocese, new configurations of ministry can emerge. It's vital now that churches are supported in more than managing difficult situations, to re-imagine how everything could fit together differently: self-supporting and local deacons and priests, Readers, pastoral assistants and local ministry development teams, incumbents and laity who pray, learn, care for one another and make courageous but carefully considered plans together.

Another radical attempt to redevelop a group of eight parishes for the current situation is described in proposals for an integrated approach to possible futures for Church and community in a large tract of rural Northumberland. *Glendale Alive* (William Temple Foundation 2008) reveals the churches' concern for the well-being of schools and caring networks and the provision of affordable housing. Clusters of parishes were intending to share resources on worship planning and the use of church buildings. Some churches were looking towards identifying ordained local ministers, Readers and other lay leaders to be trained for church and community roles. There were plans too for an overseeing and facilitating group, representative of clergy and laity and the wider neighbourhood. The initiative was rooted in a deep sense of partnership between many strands of local life. The leaders of the investigation (Bob Burston, Brian Hurst and Rob Kelsey) were seeking to 'encourage a way of working which approaches each object-ive with a world facing stance seeking first to identify and start from the spiritual needs of the people and communities' and 'for this to happen it will require a shift in mind-set by *both church and secular*' (William Temple Foundation 2008, pp. 36 and 6). The notion of clus-ters of churches sharing resources and planning together is a primary example of a relational and *episkope* re-imaging of how to be Church. The potential of such moves in many places is to bring a new energy and mobilization to churches previously dependent on stipendiary clergy and the system in which they have been pivotal.

A corporate *episkope*

There are urgent issues here around the discernment of those people and resources who can facilitate the redevelopment of an *episkope* ministry. For example, I recently had a conversation with a priest with a previous career in law. Faced with eight PCC meetings a month she had the temperament and tough-mindedness to recognize she could not and would not attend them all. A regular meeting with the vice-chairs helped them all to decide which two or three PCCs needed her specialist attention that month. This kind of detachment is essential, but it also requires the capacity to deal with the disappointment in oneself and others and to trust bishops and archdeacons to support in case of complaints. It requires networking and mentoring that on the whole is not currently on offer. Not all ordained clergy can easily manage the personal cost of such situations. I believe none should be expected to do so without networked support and focused regular opportunities for reflection, learning and spiritual development.

As I explored in *Parish Priests* (Greenwood 2009), the expanded concept of *episkope* has rich potential for reconceiving authority dynamics in local churches networked together. Ordered together, teams of laity and clergy are navigating new paths. The navigation required for an intuitive consciousness in community and individual has something of the quality portrayed in Robert Macfarlane's *The Old Ways: A journey on foot* (2012). He evokes the imagination in describing the intuitive navigational practices and dreams of those who for thousands of years have steered craft across water roads that leave no trace. There was a hidden wisdom in reading winds, birds' flight, rock types and cloud formations, and weaving together community memory and a life-and-death urgency and purpose for reaching a destination. Here he gives from Richard Kearney (2006) the gist of this inexact but truthful discernment:

> In antiquity, Irish scholars were known . . . for their practice of
> *navigatio* . . . a journey taken by boat . . . a circular itinerary of
> exodus and return . . . The aim was to undergo an apprentice-
> ship to signs of strangeness with a view to becoming more atten-
> tive to the meanings of one's own time and place – geographical,
> spiritual, intellectual.   (cited in Macfarlane 2012, p. 119)

Where priests share with and encourage in others the living out of the habits of Spirit-led gospel community, this creates an unpredictable and exhilarating life. Great courage and a willingness to take support to grow in maturity are needed for communities and priests to trust that mutual community is possible as a blessing and not as diminishing anyone.

If all Christians are to be *episkope* for others, the stipendiary priest appointed to connect and animate multiple congregations needs the self-confidence not to micro-manage but to risk trusting people and promoting their personal growth to mature ways of relating. This is to share in an extended *episkope*, showing how the community flourishes beyond belief when we leave behind individualistic patterns of working. The task requires a willingness and capacity for letting the development of self-awareness and reflection become a priority. Expectations of how a stipendiary priest will function in relation to other clergy, laity and local ministry teams will need to be more imaginative than the mechanical models often proposed.

One literary mode, magical realism, arising in art criticism through Franz Roh, helps us explore how clergy and leaders have a place that is at the same time important and not important. Magical realism aims to seize the paradox of the union of opposites. For instance, it challenges the polar opposites of life and death and the pre-colonial past versus the post-industrial present.

When laity and ordained each fully take our place, mysteriously, in a combination of lively faith and self-awareness, we are on the way to being a mature community formed in Christ. The priest, with others, exercising *episkope*, needs to know when they are working out of their own person and agenda. In this way the separate, but intimately connected, insights of the whole community of the baptized have a chance to be honoured (Thew Forrester 2003). After so many centuries of clerical dependency it is hardly surprising that, with a renewed theology of baptismal responsibility, we are in a degree of chaos.

At the induction or licensing of a new parish priest in the Church of England, the bishop pronounces, 'Receive this Cure, which is yours and mine.' This inheritance of a vicar standing in for the bishop, who is at the top of the system, must be subverted and drawn into a mutual relationship. The modelling between bishop and vicar will profoundly influence the relationship between vicar and congregation.

Representative priesthood

Every day, laity in their own spheres of life are called to demonstrate the impact of faith on their lives. One of the great tasks of forming Christian community today is to resource and stimulate laity in more confidently making faith–life connections.

The way we arrange the furniture for liturgy and learning is never neutral. It is a testing of the community's pictures of God and its operational theology. Equally, where we place ourselves in the interplay between transcendence and intimacy in our approach to God is mirrored in our ministerial authority patterns. Many clergy and people are still very content with the inherited contract, even though we have seen how this kind of representative priesthood emasculates the people of God in its response to a relational God's invitation to partnership.

The notion of representative priesthood can be actively subverted by the persistent introduction of participative authority, mutual learning styles, worship that is reciprocal – so that we 'share' Holy Communion rather than the many 'receiving' from the few. But there are two very positive aspects to the priest as representative. There is a sense in which someone with standing in the Christian community – and the wider Church, with the formation to match – is sometimes the best person to represent the gospel to the civic or retail community. But not as often as we assume. Increasingly it is possible to break through barriers that previously inhibited laity from leading funerals, visiting the sick or representing the church in schools and colleges.

There is another sense of a re-presenting priesthood. The priesthood of all the baptized is a profound element in our tradition (1 Peter 2.5–9). An *episkope* element in priesthood is to re-present to the laity their vocation and to re-present to society this role of all God's people as a matter of fact. In a time of transition there is confusion in everyone, and when we ask groups at workshops to draw up a list of what only a priest can do the variation in result is immense. The ordained in self-awareness in situations need to be asking, 'What is there that really needs my presence here?' and also 'What is the Church asking of me (and not asking) in given situations?' and 'How do I manage the credibility gap?'

Reciprocal ways of being Church are demanded by Scripture, our understanding of God's nature and plain statistics. But so many congregations have for so long been formed as mere church attenders that only clergy and office-holders hold responsibility for watching out for the Church's life. The Church as organization cannot change until we face, in ourselves and in the community as a whole, an honest fear of the radical transition that is required. Clergy in training for the overseeing role must have the support of the human disciplines of change management, psychology and a spirituality of liminality to flourish as future navigators and animators of development in their own role and that of associated groups and parishes.

The attitudes and skills required include how to engage the imagination and commitment of creative, pastorally sensitive and maturing congregations, encourage participative synergy, work with consultancy, nourish and train teams and, crucially, act as if there is already an atmosphere that welcomes new contributions (Savage and Boyd-MacMillan 2007). The parish priests now required will be naturally motivating others with maturing faith, not to pick up delegated tasks but to 'take permission' to understand and respond with their gifts to the mission of God in given situations. Infectious faith, humane practice and careful assessment of the aim to be achieved in different contexts are all vital ingredients.

Above all, the Church needs to follow the Spirit's lead in finding constructive ways of responding to the current situation in society and in the Church. I've mostly avoided some of the now rather tired language of 'shared' or 'collaborative' or 'local ministry'. Instead, through dialogue with the Jewish–Christian wisdom literature and MacIntyre's proposals for the nourishment of virtues in institutions, I am proposing the embodiment of habits that maintain and enhance the virtues that identity of the Church, where 'theory' and 'practice' meld together.

What's your investment?

So at this point it's worth stopping to ask yourself, whatever your role in church life, 'What is my interest or involvement? What have I experienced and helped to emerge in the church's life or ministry in recent times?' The variety of situations and dynamics in which priests and congregations are working extends continually. While some in cities and suburbs are still incumbents of single parishes, others have been asked to take responsibility for mission and ministry in highly complex combinations of parishes and churches. The degree of informal cooperation within clusters of churches (perhaps ecumenically) varies considerably and often depends on the – never static – chemistry between people and places. And much that can be said of the clergy has implications for Readers, lay leaders, teams and wardens.

Some would say that they are thriving while others talk more in terms of just surviving, and yet others are exhausted and demoralized. And we all may move between these states depending on our health and other personal and systemic factors. As we shall explore later, in this scenario no one is 'to blame' when individual ministers and congregations are on the edge of coping. What is at issue is that at every point the churches locally and regionally get honest about what is happening, even though 'finding solutions' cannot be achieved piecemeal. Now is the time for a seismic shift.

Churches either are very wary of management theory and practice or take to it uncritically, without sufficiently testing its operational theology. Amateur approaches to church practice built on goodwill need now to be reinforced by critical engagement with some of the more holistic organizational theories and habits. For example, the discipline of Action Inquiry can help us:

1 give an account of and recognize in ourselves the role models we have received, which are the basis of our practice;
2 be more self-aware of the power dynamics of which we are a part, catching our behaviour and deciding whether it fits well with our role in the Church;
3 find adequate and flexible language for our experience and aspirations;
4 explore periodically the situations of which we are a part where we are energized or debilitated;
5 take adequate support that fits our temperament and situation.

Time taken in regular review, alone and in our team, will:

- tell us what we have experienced;
- ask what dynamics are at work;
- discern what theology of priestly leadership is operative;
- research what secular theories could be stimulating to future practice.

The slow movement from clerical dependency

Chapters of the history of local churches have mostly been written in terms of who was the vicar and what were their theological, liturgical, pedagogical and socio-political loyalties. In short: how did they identify themselves? To appreciate how far churches have developed towards a more reciprocal culture it's worth briefly noticing some marker posts of recent times. In every era priests have defined themselves in all kinds of ways as a response to shifts in the identity and in the fortunes of public Christian practice. These have always been culturally formed, as when nineteenth-century clergy followed doctors and solicitors into professional practices and habits (see

Russell 1980), or when a confident early twentieth-century Tractarian approach, formed in semi-monastic training, placed emphasis on priestly authority, embodied in the standard wearing of cassocks and black suits, a distinct lifestyle and a focus on correctness in liturgical practice. Evangelical clergy often stressed their informality through unceremonial clothes and ways of leading worship, and were concerned not so much for church community but for individual conversion, expertise in preaching, a holy lifestyle, doctrinal knowledge and lone energy for social justice.

There have been so many shades of emphasis about priesthood over recent decades, all of them contextually formed, and all of them partial. Here are just a few examples. In the middle of the twentieth century Charles Forder, Archdeacon of York and influential author of a manual for newly ordained clergy, epitomized a confidence in a didactic teaching ministry and energetic and ordered practice (Forder 1947). In the 1960s, following pioneer Frank Lake, the founder of the Clinical Theology Association, many priests found an identity as pastoral counsellors. In the 1970s I was one who was inspired by Kenneth Leech (see Leech 1977) to regard spiritual direction as a key to unlock the lives of individual Christians and the communities in which increasingly laity were becoming leaders. David Adam's prolific writing over several decades has encouraged laity and priests together to be creative in prayer. The priest as resident theological consultant was extolled by Wesley Carr. This has produced a strong reaction from Eugene Peterson (2011), who advocates priest as preacher, teacher and one who draws people to God.

The language of sharing in ministry, with enormous variety in the ways in which this is practised, means that a corporate sense of Christian faith is now being taken for granted. The Lutheran scholar Jaroslav Pelikan concluded that the doctrine of the Church has become, in our era, the distilled concentration of the entire gospel and doctrinal memory. Theology and practice rarely fit together so neatly. Only very slowly have the insights of Vatican II and the Lima Texts and subsequent ecumenical debates on the whole people of God been seen as primary to the practice of faith.

The influence of the reappraisal of a Trinitarian experience of God

An outpouring of analogical 'social' Trinitarian writing over recent decades (e.g. Leonardo Boff, Colin Gunton and Jürgen Moltmann, Elizabeth Johnson and John Zizioulas) has gradually opened alternative pathways to inherited notions of stepped-down hierarchies. Implied in many church documents today would be an understanding of Church as a sign and mediation of the kingdom. Christian community exists through aiming to live from the quality of relations portrayed in the gospel: difference creating communion, God as an eternally generated communion of Persons. In turn such community invites the response of a new communion of persons in society and wider Creation.

The Trinity is more than the relations between divine Persons understood as individuals. It is about our being drawn into, swept up by and being part of the knowledge and goodness, the wisdom of God, for the completion of God's work in the world. Recent contributions to Trinitarian reflection emphasize the Holy Spirit's leading role among the three Persons. It is vital to exercise humility in finding language about God's 'essence' and caution in getting fixated on three-ness. What we need is the recognition of fluidity in the boundaries of the Persons, the recognition of the profusion and variation of biblical allusions to the Trinity and a care to expect an always deeper richness, lack of precision and immense complexity in considering intimacy in the divine. The Holy Spirit is more than the means of communication of the Father and the Son, but the re-creative source and heart of the divine life.

So what good news are we? Remembering the graciousness of God, instead of a culture of desperate working and competition to keep the old show on the road we can relax and recognize and celebrate the insights of others that we don't have. Pivotal is the insight that it's not all about what we do but who we are becoming, through being present to others, within the new resurrection event, that is a vital shift in all our previous apprehension of experiences, response and interactions (Jesus only gradually recognized, Luke 24.13–35; recognition and doubting simultaneously, Matthew 28.17; fear and uncertainty within faith, Mark 16.1–8; Mary only gradually 'seeing' Jesus, John 20.11–18; Jesus not recognized immediately, John 21.1–14). The base-line is that 'collaborative ministry' is not a passing fashion but a practical demonstration of gospel-shaped relationality and an expression of the true sociality that characterizes the created order.

A key to this approach is the non-negotiable proposition that isolationist and individualist approaches to ministry are contrary to the practice of Jesus' and Paul's understanding of what it means to be members 'one of another' (Romans 12.5). As Stephen Pickard (2009, chapter 9, 'One of another') notably emphasizes, it's a largely neglected insight that disciples and ministers are not only called to be Christ's body but, critically, to *animate* each other.

After hierarchy?

The pioneering social Trinitarian approaches to relational forms of ministry of the past 50 years have hardly begun to impact our paradigm of life together as Church. What must theology further unfold to resource the complex tension between the ideal of collaboration and the exercise of power in historically formed hierarchical situations?

Across the churches there is now developing a movement beyond passivity, formality, rule-keeping, legislation, institution and looking backwards. In the spirit of Chapter 1's engagement with the wisdom tradition and in the light of the renaissance of an analogical approach to the Trinity, we can move beyond some of the more rigid expression of shared or collaborative ministry. Rather than the clergy being leaders or managers of expanded ministry plans, why not consider their calling as more akin to that of seer, prophet or one appreciated for his or her prescience?

The Holy Trinity builds us up in difference and in profound mutuality actively to contribute to live together in faith, to present worship, support the growth of personal and group spirituality, accompanying all ages in learning, and to live and share faith. This emerging Church begins the urgent task of bypassing dependency on the clergy for welcoming, integrating and caring, teaching and learning on many levels to many ears, reaching out to all kinds of people and groups locally in making connections and watching out for Christian and effective ways of managing our buildings and resources.

A key task for priests and other leaders is to be helping churches constantly to check and reshape themselves in relation to a deepening awareness of God and presence with the particular situations in which they are set. It's a theological and practical task of finding and showing God's truth through the ways we perform or enact Church. What will be a constant thread in this book is how church practice can more urgently disclose the complex paradox of the significance of those called into 'holy order' within the baptized and baptizing community as a whole. Although much has been written and spoken on the sharing and collaboration between ministries, an ingrained deference to clergy remains.

A key feature of the thinking and policy-making in dioceses and parishes in recent decades has been for a Church passionately responsive to God's mission through 'collaborative' or 'every member' ministry. Advertisements for new parish incumbents mostly are couched in these terms. Yet the persistent longing for dependency within congregations is revealed in phrases that describe a heroic and energetic pastor and leader who will deliver a local church from its anxieties and make it successful. Also, the normal speech of clergy that uses possessive personal pronouns about 'my church' and 'my organist' and 'looking after' several churches is a complete give-away.

It's a reminder of the power of expectations laid down in churches over centuries when clergy were plentiful and expectations of lay discipleship were low. Theologically, the stand-alone, solo priestly ministry was a result of an overemphasis on the individual representing Christ without the monitoring effect of a sense both of being filled with the Spirit and of being directed towards the Father's kingdom. Control and subordination must be replaced by friendship, service and trust within the mystery of the Church. This book is offered as an encouragement to notice and appraise what is going on and to encourage often tentative evolutions of a new ethos and practice.

Churches now must move forward even beyond the scriptural teaching that within Christ's body there are many vital ministries. To be in conversation with the insight of the earliest Church we must learn more deeply that all ministries are a gift from both God and the Church and constantly require our focused and inevitably varying response. At the heart of this lies the passionate belief expressed by Paul that in Christ's body we who are many are one body in Christ and individually 'one of another' (Romans 12.5); without each other in mutual animation, there can be no Christian ministry.

As we shall now explore, this mutual aspiration for churches, still so fragile when deeply embedded in the local culture, is a voice that says to most people, 'You can't see yourself as a real disciples, someone who prays, can take a lead or can represent Christ in daily life in practice.' I remember well a discussion about whether we should move towards a nave sanctuary and all that this implies in liturgy and spirituality, such as standing together to share Communion. Long-standing leaders in the church had no sense of being loved, forgiven or close to God. This is a poignant reminder of the real state of so many churches and how strategies and ministry plans can make little difference until the gospel is known and received as God's blessing.

8

The unresolved dilemma

Baptismal promises and ordination vows

A collaborative approach to ministry in the body of Christ requires the capacity to move beyond the defaults we commonly observe in leadership – of autocratic or submissive behaviour. But this presumes cooperation. This seems to be innate though human beings also seem disposed to opposite behaviours. The result is we live in constant tension between these two elemental drives. (Stephen Pickard 2009, p. 3)

The road towards being ordered together

It is a vital work to represent the Church in the roles of deacon, priest and bishop, but also an essential part of the calling of the ordained and Readers is to evoke and nurture those aspects of Church in the entire *laos*. At any one time, different members of the body can exercise the foundational ecclesial aspects of bishop, priest and deacon. Although the Church is freighted with potent images of individual ministries, ecumenical conversations now invite this extended corporate notion of these ministries to flourish.

Although in the 1980s many of us were fired up at the notion of every baptized person sharing in Christ's ministry, theologians such as Paul Avis and John Collins have persuasively invited us to see discipleship, rather than ministry, as essentially connected with baptism. This is partly because ministry has always a mutual quality, given by the community and received by the commissioned person within mutually agreed conditions. All ministries are concerned with servanthood and humility, so it is not right to see the deacon and diaconal ministries as bottom of a hierarchy of those who lord it over others. Deaconing is essentially being authorized and sent on an urgent mission, perhaps of evangelism, teaching or social justice.

Lumen Gentium, the key Vatican II text, spoke of the structure of Church as marked by episcopal collegiality. It can be confusing to Anglicans that the Roman Catholic Church regards the diocese as the 'local church' focused in and constituted by the bishop. But what matters here is the notion that a diocese is not just an administrative unit of the wider Church, but in itself the full organic embodiment of the universal Church of Christ. This is a distinct move away from regarding a diocese or local church as a separate bit of an organization under a single ruler, but instead as part of a family, communion or field of episcopal churches.

Our long history with bishops, as clerical aristocrats above criticism, hinders our acceptance that all share in the calling in some way or other to represent the work of Christ through a shared watching out, *episkope*. There's a great deal of work to unpack what it could mean to be one of another, ministries ordered together in love, regardless of any financial implications. Malcolm Grundy (2011) has made a magnificent start in terms of exploring the practice of bishops working collegially, rather than as solo performers in their separate territories. There is more to be done to unlock further the *episkope* theory–practice of clergy and teams in situations of many kinds, connecting more overtly with those exercising the office of bishop. This will have role and diary implications for everyone concerned.

Priests for building the Church in its habits

I have personally valued and had many opportunities to learn and grow through my own four decades of ordained ministry. One of my most significant teachers in recent years is the Franciscan, Richard Rohr. Living with paradox, he claims, is something that appears to be a contradiction, but from another perspective is not a contradiction at all. It allows for every profound truth

> to be countered by another, and usually less flattering, profound truth. You and I are living paradoxes, which everybody except ourselves can see. If you can hold and forgive the contradictions within yourself, you can normally do it everywhere else, too.
> (Rohr in Finley *et al.* 2012)

Holding the balance between the priesthood of all and that of the ordained is still an unresolved matter for churches generally. Sometimes, in writing and leading workshops, to enhance the role of all the baptized I have tended to undervalue the very particular discernment processes, formation and solemn vows (varying through the years with the wording of the ordinal) undertaken by the ordained.

If we can separate out the notion of being part of the ordering of the Church from issues of personality and preference it helps us move beyond a misunderstanding of 'equality' that assumes, for example, that if two ordained or licensed ministers are leading worship they must each lead 50 per cent. When we simply operate at the level of personality, maturity and temperament, then all kinds of disputes occur about who has permission to do this or that, who walks where in processions and how the liturgy is divided up 'fairly' between clergy, Readers and laity. Taking the relationality of the Trinity in which no one is diminished through communion and mutual love, the ordering of Church in courtesy but clarity offers a way forward, though as we note elsewhere this requires us to be subversive to show that the baptized and Readers are not second-best to clergy. It also requires a degree of internal human self-respect and confidence as well as the respect of leaders and peers for this to become just what we are as Church.

The promissory character of solemn ordination vows loses none of its potency when it is held in tension with baptism promises. The general lack of preparation for baptism and the diversity of ways in which this sacrament is entered into and lived out make it difficult to compare with the narrow gate of ordination. Support and worship and learning options for baptism families, and a renewed emphasis on formation in discipleship for all ages, is offering some chance for rebalancing. But currently the Church's disproportionate attention to ordination over baptism adds to a picture of a society where the practice of faith is becoming a private world of those who exercise that spiritual choice.

The role of the ordained is a vital resource for the inspiring and drawing out of the gifts of the whole Church. To be truly animators of Church, clergy, rather than being set apart, are set within the Church as disciples with everyone else; but they are also given permission and responsibility to draw out vitality and new possibilities in the local church. Priests in the local church have the primary task of helping all the baptized re-member their place within the community, as having assigned tasks, roles and significance for the whole. Clergy can't vicariously do the work of the body and they must resist the seductive temptation to pretend that if they act as providers of worship, care and evangelism, this is the practice the Church requires.

Stipendiary, self-supporting and house-for-duty priests, with deacons and Readers, are called together to draw people to know Christ in the Spirit and to recognize the gifts of others as well as of themselves. Regardless of remuneration, radically, everyone's ministry is given by and built up by all the others. We gradually learn to animate one another, to be tied up in each other's ministries through pain and conflict but hopefully also in joy. The demolition of myths surrounding the special place of the ordained is made possible by remembering the particular Christian take on vulnerability, sin and the possibilities of restoration. The emphasis on servanthood, unless combined with Jesus' invitation to us to be friends, can unintentionally distort relationships, especially where women or marginalized people get further hurt in an institutionalized polarization of servant–served relationships. In the New Testament church, service and friendship are inseparable and can help us now to follow Christ's own fragile and demanding ministry.

The wisdom of the ordinal?

As communities grow in confidence as Church in all whose faith is lively, the number of vocations to ordained, stipended and self-supporting ministry will increase. It is, however, increasingly vital that the Church gives clear messages in recruiting and forming the ordained that there are very different opportunities and demands on clergy in different roles. David Heywood (2011) has robustly emphasized the needs for a reappraisal of formation for priests.

Expressing and mediating the corporate nature of the Church.

The invisible representational dimension of priesthood has been the heartbeat of Anglicanism, evidenced in thousands of deeply moving and profoundly sacrificial priestly lives (see Samuel Wells and Sarah Coakley 2008). The present exploration of a vision of priesthood as relational, as a resource to the work of the whole people of God, continues by a brief reflection on the ordination of priests. The event of ordination is increasingly an act of the whole Church, even though laity in sending parishes (except for locally ordained ministry) are consulted mainly through the consent of the parochial church council and character references.

Those who have been ordained as deacon, priest or bishop have undergone a series of finely tuned and carefully administered processes: discernment, formation, training, appointment and licensing to a particular place and the performance of the liturgy of ordination (ordinal). The bishop only proceeds to call down the Holy Spirit for the gifts needed in ordination after the candidates have been publicly presented as suitable for and accepting of their calling, intellectually, spiritually and temperamentally. Increasingly there is an assumption that the ordained have not completed their learning but are committed to a lifetime's personal and vocational development. The Church's *koinonia* wisdom is that no one is ordained in isolation or to a status that does not also have a daily commitment to the core values and habits of the Church.

What the verbs and performance in the liturgy reveal of the Church's expectation of priesthood today

The opening words of the bishop begin in a very corporate mutual mood. In the introduction of the *Common Worship Ordinal* of the Church of England, priests are called to re-present to the whole Church their calling to be disciples of Christ and God's people who know and proclaim God's love. Priestly ordination is to remind and build up the faithful community, nurtured by the Holy Spirit to witness to God's love and to work for the coming of his kingdom. This work, shared with the bishop, clergy and others, is 'to sustain the community of the faithful by the ministry of word and sacrament, that we all may grow into the fullness of Christ and be a living sacrifice acceptable to God'.

However, at the time of ordination the bishop delivers to the congregation and the candidates an overwhelming list of priestly acts to be undertaken for the sake of individuals and the Church as a whole. The ordinal also places a strong emphasis on the priest being 'sent' in a solo, Christological sense, to proclaim and watch, to be messengers, watchmen and stewards of the Lord; their calling includes teaching, admonishing, feeding and providing for God's family, searching out the lost and guiding them through confusions for their salvation. They are to call their hearers to repentance and to declare in Christ's name the absolution and forgiveness of their sins.

The list continues mainly with more activity towards others: telling (though with all God's people), baptizing, walking with, nurturing, unfolding the Scriptures, preaching, declaring, presiding at the Lord's table, leading his people in worship, offering with them, blessing, resisting evil, supporting, defending, interceding, ministering, preparing the dying. Finally the emphasis moves, as 'guided by the Spirit, they are to discern and foster the gifts of all God's people, that the whole Church may be built up in unity and faith'.

Then the ordinands are required very rightly to dedicate themselves to practices that will strengthen their following of Jesus: accepting an Anglican interpretation of Scripture, and being devoted to prayer and study. There follows the expectation that priest and people will learn together how to proclaim everywhere the good news. There is a strong note of dependency in the description of the priest 'ministering the doctrine and sacraments of Christ' so that those in their charge may be kept from error.

There follow more personal and family commitment vows that emphasize the exemplar notion of ordination. The subsequent vow significantly insists on cooperation with the laity for the work of the kingdom.

Order in a virtue ecclesiology

All this is a reminder of the continuing dilemma of holding in difference and equal value the 'lay' and the ordained. Undoubtedly, I have experienced personally and with others the profound potency of the majestic event of an ordination. This whirl of grandiosity is a vital psychological support at the start of a demanding new calling within the Church. And yet so often the very performance of the liturgy or ordination and the choreography devastates the continuing work of recognizing the high significance of baptism.

Equally I have known the power of a baptism in the Sunday liturgy or at the dawn Easter Vigil. Samuel Wells (2011, chapter 1) notes that in the thanksgiving over the water in the rite of baptism the Holy Spirit is mentioned five times. This Spirit given to all God's people is certainly for personal blessing but is also given to persons together as the body of Christ living in giftedness (1 Corinthians 12.7–11), experiencing the gifts (1 Corinthians 13.1–3, 13) and displaying the fruits (Galatians 5.22–23) of the Spirit.

The combination of the ordinal text (with the unselfconscious clerical power of cathedral events in former monastic buildings) and a still weak sense of baptismal gifting and responsibility leaves a great deal more exploration to be done on how we perform both baptism and ordination services so that any sense of competition for love and attention is eliminated. However, given all that we now perceive about the importance of symbolism, language and kinaesthetic learning, we have to ask whether in fact this liturgy obscures rather than proudly presents a notion of priesthood to which increasingly many subscribe.

In his consideration of episcopal vows, Pickard (2009, chapter 13, 'This is your promise') identifies the dissonance between the solemn promises and the expectations and requirements of the contemporary Church. The vows may be good in themselves but they are designed for a Church that no longer exists.

Clergy now faced with the complex and often heart-breaking tasks of overseeing almost overwhelming situations, not least multi-benefice situations, could with justification say that the ordination service does not articulate or support just what is now being called from them. As a Church we cannot seriously continue to be satisfied with the dissonance between emerging practice of the Church and its ministries and the ordinal as it currently stands.

The wisdom of a Trinitarian ecclesiology is that intensity of contact with God and commitment to the kingdom can exist endlessly in infinite situations. Pickard's discussion of priestly vows offers particular stimulus to liturgists, educators, spiritual companions and bishops in their responsibility for articulating and enacting the process of becoming and remaining ordained.

The practices required in a virtue ecclesiology must recognize the fragile, passionate, 'one of another' character of a church in which participants, in friendship, serve God's mission. Here is encouragement to be consistently innovative and courageous for bishops and all seriously engaged in evoking or leading reflective Christian ministry.

9

Virtues and habits of churches and priests

Taking responsibility together for being Church

A virtue ecclesiology would look carefully at the *motives* behind planning, strategy, and structural organization, with a view to emphasizing the priority of love. A virtue ecclesiology might enable Christians to explore in a comparative fashion what sort of communities their churches are in reality and what they aspire to be, in accordance with the gospel and the rich traditions of Christianity.   (Gerard Mannion 2007, p. 227)

Partnership between local churches and the diocese

My aim here is to support and encourage the gradual awakening to a more corporate and mutual way of doing Church within which clergy are significant animators. So the question, 'Are there generic virtues to which any single or group of churches might aspire?' will always need to come long before 'What is the priest to do?' Though having said that, and given our history of dependence on the ordained as carrying and growing the wisdom of the Church, it will often be precisely from the clergy that such profound moves will originate.

The Church in Wales Review, commissioned in 2011, faced that it could not and should not continue its present practice into the future. An external report, written consultatively, makes major strategic proposals for a future where increasingly parishes are being configured together and the number of available stipendiary priests further diminishes. It takes as the base-line that the present system is no longer sustainable, that local churches can find a new self-confidence in the gifts they have for discipleship and ministry, and that a new era of cooperation between clergy and laity can be born.

As with all such reviews, the question is how this report's many 'shoulds' will come to pass. Such proposals, acclaimed on publication as 'the solution', routinely falter when the implementation is not given the proportion of resources that will give it the chance to make an impact on business as usual.

To achieve their chosen virtues, what are the habits to be enacted by communities and animated by clergy and others in leadership? What are the habits for people and clergy so that clusters of parishes can together aspire to virtues that will advance the kingdom in their situation? And, following MacIntyre, how can dioceses and local churches look for excellence in the practices that identify their chosen values, at every point of contact with others?

Avoiding the fixed language of models and strategies, and as much as possible the term 'leadership', I shall be identifying from my own and others' experience questions and ways of naming and practising some of the habits required. The virtues chosen by any church will depend on its long-term goal. God has given us all the gifts we need. A local church or group of ministers can light a bonfire of hope and discover in the process something so vital and engaging that it can draw people to the light of Christ. Then others see the flames and the smoke and feel the heat enough to come and see and to ask good questions and scale over ideas to be redeveloped in a new locality. This is a permanent state so that change is normal, not unwelcome crisis management. And the bishop's staff team's energies must be directed towards creating a safe environment for local churches to experiment and try new paths.

Dioceses will need to risk investing confidently in a commissioned team – not just an individual person – who on behalf of all watch out for and pay sharp attention to new initiatives. Such a team with sensitivity can see the potential for new virtues and habits, in partnership with 'normal' working, to 'scale across' within the diocese or beyond. The bishop in watching out will attempt to steer that from becoming another control mechanism; the method of support has to match the hesitant and fragile nature of a new virtue or habit.

Team-working in families, sports, politics, economics and all human fields of activity is widely recognized now as a key to significant accomplishment and growth. A diocesan team for the sustainable development of a new aspect or concept of its life needs permission to act responsibly in helping churches to live simultaneously with foundational stability and transformational disequilibrium. The social networking and community of methods of Action Inquiry suggest seven characteristics of uniting the stability of an organization with the risky chaos essential to development in new circumstances. These theoretical proposals for a Foundational Community of Inquiry can seem almost mystical in their particular language and frame of reference. They resonate in many ways with the wisdom– virtue ecclesiology we have explored so far:

- Appreciation of the continuing interweaving of opposites to make a whole: action–research, sex–politics, past–future, symbolic– diabolic, etc.
- Continuing, empirical and experiential research on relations between spiritual–intuitive vision, theoretical–practical strategy, timely performing and assessing outcomes in the visible, external world.
- Fundamentalist, universal ideologies are challenged by emphases on peer mutuality among people of different backgrounds and on the humble, vulnerable practice of timely Action Inquiry.
- Political friction between different paradigms/frames/actionlogics within the organization and between the organization and the wider environment.
- Collaborative enquiry structure fails when it does not meet the alchemical challenge of timely transformational, liberating, collective action.
- If timely transformational collective action is taken, shared purpose is revealed as sustaining and as generating multiple choices for action (and feedback on the consequences of such choices) from all participants.
- New experiences of time: his-story, becomes my-story; interplay of time-bound needs, timeless archetypes and timely creative enquiry.

Communities of practice–enquiry learn the virtue of paying equal attention to the quality of their handling of finance, politics, resources and spirituality. They cannot function without a long-term commitment to the personal transformation of their participants. What if, over the next four generations of the twenty-first century, church leaders and communities begin to seek support for their development towards the characteristics of at least the *strategist* in Torbert's 'action-logics' (see pages 41–3)? And what if, instead of adversarial binary argument, they come to value integrity, mutuality and sustainability in the transformational ways of Action Inquiry?

As we have seen, normal working and innovation do not function in the same way. In making provision for a diocesan or regional team to exercise an *episkope* function for opening a good space for innovations to be appreciated and further developed, not dictating what it should look like everywhere, questions that need to be considered include:

- Besides the leader, who is needed on the team? Should they come from inside or outside the diocese? Can dioceses increasingly pool resources despite their differing cultures?
- Does everyone involved in overseeing the innovation initiative need to be available full time? Can some sustain their existing responsibilities?
- How should the team be organized? How does this differ from 'normal' working?
- What specific conflicts are likely to arise between the innovation initiative and continuing routines? How can they be anticipated and resolved? Where is the bishop in all this?
- To whom should the team report? What are the supervisor's most important responsibilities and critical challenges?

Church as a Christian organization

'What is a diocese apart from its local churches?' lies behind many disputes about clergy, buildings, money or land. It's often the case that we have great aspirations for Church as community but sigh with frustration or get angry with Church as 'institution' ('them', the 'diocese' or 'the Bishop'). One of MacIntyre's insights is that the virtues of an organization could be expected to flourish in every dimension of the organization. The Durham University Receptive Ecumenism initiative addresses this under the heading 'practice-institution'. That is an exploration of how once a local church is networked it inevitably gets 'institutionalized' and how far in that process it can still portray habits that are recognizably Christian. The Receptive Ecumenism researchers asked two key questions of local church members, related to but looser than a strictly MacIntyrean approach:

- How would you describe the main elements of your faith?
- How does the institutionalization of the Church affect the practice of faith in your case?

The argument for studying the Church in this way is that MacIntyre's conceptual framework is at a relatively early stage of development in relation to the study of organizations, with limited empirical testing already carried out in general and with none, apart from the Receptive Ecumenism studies, on Church as an organization. Case study research is a vital way of testing the value of MacIntyre's theory in this context.

At the end of the interview participants were invited to score their church in terms of the degree to which it is 'institutionalized' on a scale of 1–5, where 1 is highly institutionalized, 3 is moderately institutionalized and 5 is un-institutionalized. A following question asked whether the effect of the institutionalized church was 1 – very supportive, 2 – supportive, 3 – neutral, 4 – unsupportive or 5 – very unsupportive to the practice of faith.

Varying themes emerged from the research through responses to the questions on the main elements of the faith of those questioned and the extent to which they were borne out in the practices of Church as institution. They included:

- a sense of being loved by God, along with the whole human race, and being invited into co-working for God's final purposes for Creation;
- a personal sense of calling into relationship with God in Christ, leading to the call to mission and worship and the growth of the kingdom;
- a very personal and individual relationship with God, leading to salvation and reception into heaven;
- a belief that faith statements would differ but unite around a Trinitarian understanding of God.

There were both differences and similarities across denominational borders about to what extent belief was connected with practical action. The overall conclusion from the analysis was that there is no obvious agreement across the denominations on what the core practices of faith might be. Respondents sometimes connected their reasons for the impetus for practical action with their own sense of final purpose. The formality of some of the replies led to speculation on the influence of the formulas of an institution on personal commitment statements. This was not a denial of the personal belief of those concerned but a suggestion that a degree of institutional influence gave shape to the theological content of the responses.

Virtues and habits in local churches

Local churches or groups of churches need to give time to considering what is their overall long-term aim or purpose, and the virtues and habits to foster them lies at a deeper level than making lists of tasks and responsibilities. This process need to be continuous and at all kinds of levels. Far more must be done together as churches abandon isolationism and learn to be 'one of another'. The following is a list of some of the ways in which churches could use processes to discover and communicate their virtues and practices:

1 a series of open evening conversations on the theme 'Who is our God?'
2 accepting the diocesan challenge to draw up and keep revising a Mission Action Plan;
3 shaping every church council meeting around core virtues and habits – which are adapted in changing circumstances and as people are able to give time and energy;
4 although a church council will vary in how much time is given to looking at each virtue from meeting to meeting, the fact that they are all laid out in the agenda each time they meet roots the virtues and habits into the common consciousness and awareness;
5 using the Annual Report and Annual Meeting to be more than a record of business but a celebration of the practice of habits;
6 communication in sermons, magazine letters and the development of a website;

7 several churches in a cluster or deanery sharing an administrator for finance, printing, wedding preparation, accepting funerals;

8 a discipleship and ministry celebration day, where instead of coffee after the morning Eucharist a simple lunch surrounded by stalls can be used to explain how progress is being made in the various practices and to attract new helpers, e.g. for Godly Play, Messy Church or Justice and Peace;

9 courses of induction and learning;

10 liturgy – frequently spelling out and celebrating in the Sunday liturgy pieces of work in which groups have been involved, e.g. a WaterAid project for Sierra Leone, Street Pastors or a food bank project;

11 visitors from the wider Church who give the local church a chance to explain itself;

12 occasional half-days or weekends when we invite a facilitator to work with leaders;

13 a year of saying 'Yes', when 12 members of the congregation meet regularly to pray, read Scripture and have conversations about God's call to their church;

14 banners made up of photographs and short phrases that, by hanging in church, are a reminder to everyone of the key themes by which the church aims to live.

Community of blessing

The interweaving of the wisdom tradition and virtue ecclesiology offers a way to hold in respect the mutual contributions of those we call 'lay' with those of the ordained, denigrating neither. The notion that each brings a blessing to the other is such a profound and generous strand within Scripture and Christian practice at its best.

Blessing by and for those steeped in faith was the punctuation of the infancy narratives in Luke. Mary is told 'blessed is the fruit of your womb' (Luke 1.42); filled with the Holy Spirit at the birth of John, the priest Zechariah blesses God; the wise old one Simeon blesses God for the birth of Jesus and blesses Mary and Joseph. At the end of Luke's Gospel, Jesus at Bethany 'lifting up his hands . . . blessed them' (Luke 24.50). The term 'them' has been used through the chapter from the reference to the 'eleven and their companions' (Luke 24.33) gathered in Jerusalem. In the closing verses of Luke's Gospel Jesus blesses those present at Bethany; while he is blessing them he withdraws and is carried to heaven; finally they worship Jesus and returning joyfully to Jerusalem continue to bless God in the temple. This is the blessing and commissioning of a group of young people, filled with the promise of the Spirit, ready to serve the kingdom.

We are aware today of so many challenges to our faith and the need to be open to receiving blessings in order to be a blessing to others. As we have explored earlier, utterly central to being Church is a Spirit-led relationship with God the Holy Trinity. Faith is the gift of a God-centred ecology of blessing. Blessings from God circulate throughout Creation (Genesis 12.1–3): God blesses us within all Creation; we bless God; we give blessings to one another; all Creation blesses God; and we bless Creation. Blessing, praising and giving thanks to God is the lifeblood of the psalms.

Blessing is not amorphous but particular to occasions and relationships. The accounts of David being chosen and anointed as King in Israel – with echoes now in coronations and consecrations, baptisms and ordinations – are a prime illustration of blessing as a procedure for discerning what blessings are right for people and whether to bless people into particular responsibilities. Churches, well aware of the tensions around these discernment processes today, are asking:

- Who is considered fit to carry the burden of being an incumbent or bishop?
- How far are gender and sexual orientation to be factors?
- What kinds of intelligence are needed for particular roles?
- How well will this person respect and cooperate with others?
- Is this one right for this set of circumstances at this point of development in this set of diverse communities?

Scripture shows God to be the ultimate source of blessings but they come mostly through other people: parents, friends, spouses, spiritual guides, teachers and wise ones.

Priest as interpreter

Gratitude for blessings is an essential part of receiving the blessing and often leads to taking on more responsibility. But Scripture and experience remind us of the cost of being blessed into particular works of leadership. One of the leadership callings (for laity and clergy) within Christian community is to be wise interpreters of Scripture and tradition, learning how to draw on treasures from the past (Matthew 13.52). Those blessed into authorized ministries must help their communities become a wise blessing.

I am stressing over and over my conviction that local church communities, in whatever networks are most natural, need to confidently own and practise their virtues for the kingdom. Here, for example, are six virtues into which to grow:

- being grounded in God;
- being formed through Scripture and Eucharist;
- choosing to be open and caring;
- setting off on pilgrimage;
- cultivating an integrating wholeness;
- communicating in multiple ways.

These are generic virtues that could be opened up in endless contexts through the adoption of some of the habits outlined in this book, scaled across to different situations.

In my discussions of the themes of this book with many others, the vital work of the parish priest as 'interpreter' has emerged. An essential part of my work is to watch, listen and attend to what is going on and how my being part of it has an influence. It seems important to have someone, never isolated but identifiable, who has permission to re-present back and forwards, in church and the wider community, what seems to be happening or emerging and to ask questions, to speak the thanks for the community and the value placed on pieces of ministry by others. This interpreting minister also has to have the courage to say, 'You must be joking!' or 'Up with this we will not put!' or 'If you continually talk for 80 per cent of every meeting, have you not noticed the effect you are having?'

Fortunately, just as the three orders are aspects of Church and not exclusive to those who hold public office, there are 'lay' people (the Simeons and Annas) who offer wise blessings and interpretations, often requiring courage, for us to receive with thanksgiving. Throughout my own time as a priest I have known women and men who saw God as the source of their very being and as the communicator of wisdom they needed for daily life. This quality is given a prominence within black majority churches from which we could learn. Eva Hill Rowntree describes how her life had been enriched in great measure through conversations with 'those who had already gained from others and from life'. She sees it as urgent for herself to pass on wisdom: 'We're in a brand new day of the Web, information oversaturation, HIV/AIDS, violence, family conflicts and break-ups, you name it. So, there are special needs calling for extraordinary wisdom' (Streaty Wimberly and Parker 2002, p. 15).

Exercising our role as a Reader or a priest understood as 'interpreter' requires in us a high degree of self-awareness and commitment to mutuality. We need to know in our bones that the 'it' that is our role can only truly be exercised in mutual accountability. We need the inner confidence and courage to allow others to challenge us within the respectful ordering of community. Bishop David Jenkins has often reminded us that those who develop a taste for prophecy should immediately give it up. It should no longer be the case that clergy, through our own limitations, can inhibit the flow of debate or limit the possibilities of communities to what we can accept or manage.

10

Spirit-led community

Growing in hospitality and love through sharing in the Eucharist

> Divine freedom, like human freedom, is achieved in communion. The Spirit is the freedom of God permeating, animating, quickening, incorporating, affiliating, engrafting, consummating, the creature out of love. The movements of the Spirit of God cannot be controlled, domesticated, or regulated, but the presence of the Spirit can clearly be observed where there is *koinonia*.
> (Catherine Mowry LaCugna 1991, p. 299)

Practising a virtue ecclesiology

A virtue ecclesiology is possible when every point of its scope and every office-holder engages with the core practices and seeks excellence in performing them. An essential strand of this book's argument is that the whole *laos*, ordered together and also in particular orders, flourishes through building Christ's Church in virtues and practices that serve God's kingdom. My own persuasion is that becoming a community, focused on but not limited by the Eucharist, is a key practice of a virtue ecclesiology. I fully respect that others will choose different priorities for building relational virtues. What is true for the local church has to be equally true for the diocesan staff and administration who must sustain the wider Church in productive practices that build the chosen virtues of the diocese.

This is a move from regarding the institutional life of the Church with some embarrassment, as at best a necessary evil. It will inevitably involve conversations that go beyond normal synod business and a different pace of institutional life that has some chance of moving from delivering only more of the same. There has to be an agreed good purpose for the entire enterprise that goes further than 'keeping the show on the road a while longer'. Everyone has a need to know and be able to say what is this good purpose and what are the excellent ways in which it is happening in practice. This needs to be a mantra, poster, narrative, song, drama and prayer, but not one simply delivered 'from the top' or without effective debate. It will have internal goods that build up the community in faith, worship and evangelism, but will also be proud to have external goods such as being well known and respected for its practices and being attractive to newcomers, as well as helping people to integrate into the community.

A virtue ecclesiology will be vigilant that it does not remain satisfied with merely external goods to the neglect of people giving their hearts to God in contemplation and to the world's poor in social action. True innovation, that goes beyond report writing, is costly in time, resources and emotional energy. It requires belief and risk-taking at every point of the institutional compass. It requires in its practitioners the humility to keep checking their own self-awareness through Action Inquiry and mentoring.

To move from a fixed-order, predetermined Church to be open to the Spirit's leading now means regularly asking the Triple Loop questions (see page 42) about purpose, aspiration and God's calling, listening to the location, and only then asking what virtues are needed and how we should practise them. What quality of gospel community do we need to be and what practices will best serve this outcome? The calling of this community in this place at this time must be a prior consideration to the kind of institution we belong to. The form of a local church must suit its purpose just as the architecture of a building should articulate and facilitate its particular function.

A poem of Mary Oliver's, 'The Hermit Crab' (2010, pp. 36f.), describes the ocean as depositing on the shore the detritus that it does not require as, with the turning tide, it rolls onwards to newness. The Holy Spirit helps churches discern what to leave behind as we seek the next stage in our destiny. The Holy Spirit gives us courage to unclench our fingers from what has been a vital and dear support to us until now. The Holy Spirit gives us habits in which Christians can be formed together in the body of Christ.

A Church that walks with Jesus will, like him, embody kingdom virtues. The Spirit led Jesus to rely only on *abba* and finally in resurrection gives us life of an unbelievable character for a new era into which the Spirit is drawing us. This can only mean breaking with traditional practices. To be Church in a new era requires us to focus intensely on God in praise and thanksgiving. At his Ascension Jesus commissioned the disciples to continue his work with his blessing and later they received the same Spirit he had received at his baptism.

It is the experience of the Church that to be created and maintained in virtues, performed in a variety of ways, vitally there need to be the practices of recognizing, educating and directing spiritual gifts 'for building up the body of Christ' and making a united people (Ephesians 2.15). We often fail, get overtired and misunderstand one another and through the Spirit find our way again. The Spirit brings love, joy, patience, kindness, generosity, faithfulness, gentleness and self-control (Galatians 5.22–23). In other words, wherever the Spirit is at work, fruit just bursts out in abundance 'as unearned gift' (Wells 2006, pp. 48f.).

Churches must learn the conviction that in and through the Holy Sprit the Christian community has been given the task of proclaiming and commending and following the way of Jesus' true and good news about the relation of the world to the Father. Church does not possess the truth as the truth but through face-to-face listening and communicating with Jesus as a person. A mother with two young boys was drawn with her friend and her children into informal Sunday afternoon worship. They're now all preparing for baptism and confirmation. Nicola has joined the planning group for the informal worship and insists that she would never have come back after her first visit if she had felt talked *at* rather than talked *with*. She reminds us to speak with adults and children at their eye level. This is moving from relevance towards presence and authenticity, and engaging.

Examples of chosen practices

What would be a central practice of Church? As already discussed, although some might say celebrating the Eucharist, others might prefer making new disciples or establishing and maintaining or 'forming' Christian community (Ephesians 4.2 and 2.15). So, for example, if a church identified forming Christian community as a central practice, how would it unfold in sub-practices? Moore (2012, p. 55) reports on the work of Nancey Murphy and James McClendon, listing practices of what it takes for Church to be Church:

- *Worship* This will be characterized by conversation initiated by God, including public prayer, sacraments, Scripture reading and responding in preaching; it will include penitence and reconciliation with others, an overcoming of all forms of exclusion and separation.
- *Witness* This will include evangelistic preaching, door-to-door visiting, local revival and global mission.
- *Works of mercy* These will continue Jesus' ministry among the poor, the sick and the excluded, and as a consequence, pastoral care.
- *Discipling* This will be through public teaching, formation of individual Christians and the exercise of church discipline.
- *Discernment* This is a complex social practice involving testing spirits to see if they are from God, recognizing authentic prophecy, expecting the Holy Spirit's guidance regarding mission and making corporate policies.
- *Eucharist* McLendon places the 'covenant meal' as a central practice in community formation, essentially moral and ethical but essential to the shaping of common life.

In adapting the academic discourse on what might be called practices or sub-practices, my own intuition and experience is that the notion of a small number of practices to serve a 'virtuous' Church's final purpose has potential for releasing new energy in re-imagining Church. However, we are in danger of returning to a blueprint mentality unless we recognize how context requires that proposals be adapted and categorized, worked out through a varying range of language, habits and practices of varying complexity.

The following are practices that celebrate and unfurl the virtues of abundance, difference and uncertainty: making new disciples; baptizing; praying; sharing life, faith and pains together; welcoming strangers and serving the marginalized, as a blessing; witnessing to God's truth; pursuing social justice; exercising pastoral care; making provision for learning, spiritual development, growth in discernment or wisdom. Simply, but not without great care, this involves clergy and colleagues helping local churches to firmly set a 'tone' that people warm to, enjoy and are proud to tell others about. All of this is encapsulated in the Church's core practice, the celebration of the Eucharist.

As an adverbial comment on this list, the *way in which these prac-tices are performed* is as vital to achieving the virtue. So learning will be mutual, relationships respectful, people clear about the boundar-ies of their assigned tasks, all ages equally respected and each aspect of being Church measured by all that Jesus showed of the Father's love.

Christian wisdom formation has its source in God. It relies on our faith in God, openness to God, discernment of God's desire for our lives, and a commitment to let ourselves be drawn into com-panionship with God through corporate disciplines and practices such as individual and group study of Scripture, prayer, contempla-tion, journal writing, participating in worship and retreats, inten-tional conversations with spiritual guides, listening to, creating and responding to music and creativity, and repentance and fasting.

One thing for certain is that God wants everyone to join in, to learn more about themselves, to feel at home in God's house, and to know what it is to live with each other and with God, what it is to be Church.

How does worship involve us in God's loving gift of truth and holi-ness? What kind of wisdom results? Some of the respondents in the Receptive Ecumenism interviews spoke about the importance for them of worship that reveals diversity of belief and opinion: 'I like the ways we worship in the Salvation Army; I like the joy and the music and the style'; 'A part of my faith is about meeting together with other Christians, meeting together for worship' (United Reformed Church); 'Worship, prayer and Bible study, that kind of thing, cor-porately and individually within our church there are lots of areas where we can meet together' (Salvation Army).

Within this survey, the practices of meeting, hearing, responding, sharing and going (Wells 2006) were to some extent in evidence, but focused on corporate prayer and preaching/hearing the preached word. Scripture emerged as a significant term in its own right, both as authoritative in individuals' lives and as something they studied indi-vidually and together. Liturgy also emerged as a related term, provid-ing the structure within which worship could be conducted, 'so for me the corporate institution of the church, my relationship with the bishop and through the bishop with the collegiality of the bishops, the sacraments and the liturgy of the Church is hugely important' (Anglican).

Wisdom in intensity and extensity

The links between intense knowing of God through worship and prayer make it possible for churches to extend their knowing and working with God into the whole of life, for the world's transformation. The Trinitarian God, known in the detail of life, is described by Daniel W. Hardy as a crucible of holiness, a refining fire evoking fear, hope, love, hatred, desire, joy, sorrow, gratitude, compassion and zeal, God's holiness persisting through suffering to death and burning away fragmentation between human beings (2001, pp. 16f.). It's what Hardy used to call 'full Christianity'. What would it be like if all Christians fully lived the life of Christ in every part of human reality?

In baptism God's life in the world and our new life in Christ are dramatically drawn together. At Pentecost the disciples were changed when the intensity of God's resurrection, previously unknown, re-orientating life in Christ, came violently into contact with God's life extended within all Creation (Acts 2.1–11). Filled with the Holy Spirit, the disciples were given the ability to communicate God's power in ways that could be understood by all. They participated in resurrection life and they extended its benefit to many others. This is what is Church, the dynamic of knowing Christ in a concentrated way at the same time as making Christ widely known. The early Christian community found new confidence and energy and were visible:

- spending much time in the temple;
- breaking bread from house to house;
- eating with glad and generous hearts;
- praising God;
- having the goodwill of all the people;
- and day by day the Lord was adding to their number those who were being saved. (Acts 2.46–end).

Their worship was characterized by intense praise and the meal by which Jesus had connected them with his suffering, death and resurrection. Celebrating this in generosity creates an extending atmosphere of goodwill. This growing intensity also made present the same righteousness of God that Jesus had embodied so people were drawn to recognize their sinfulness, repentance, baptism and receiving the gift of the Holy Spirit (Acts 2.37–38). Similarly this new intensity pervaded their life together (Acts 2.43–45). They were bound together in recognizing each other's needs and sharing in common practical and economic means of life. In this way they came to a deeper sense of who they were and what had happened to them (Acts 4.8–12). They had become a learning community – seeking a body of knowledge that was wisdom rather than information.

This new learning was shaped in and demonstrated by new worship, a sense of God's righteousness that they had experienced in face-to-face encounter with Jesus, a common life and a sharing of reflection. Luke in Acts is not just telling us the facts of what happened at Pentecost and beyond but offering a narrative that invites churches in all ages to live in a wisdom that is simultaneously demanding and an exhilarating taste of the new life Christ brings.

Celebrating the Eucharist

In *Being God's People* (Greenwood and Hart 2011), Sue Hart and I explored the virtues and practices of Christian community through the rhythm and texture of the Eucharistic gathering. Here are eight practices that illustrate ways of celebrating the Eucharist that could ventilate Christian community identity. In different situations, how could some of this give renewed focus to the community's intense engagement with God?

1 The sense of expectation – a sense of readiness that comes through careful preparation, calmness mixed with anticipation in the 30 minutes before the worship, energetically watching out for those who have been sick or for visitors and newcomers, having a group wash and prepare vessels the day before, setting out books and bread and wine in good time so as to leave open the nave sanctuary space, free from the distraction of servers and clergy moving or talking there as people arrive.

2 Awareness of the physical space – giving great thought, consulting, planning and fund-raising to allow the eucharistic space to hold together transcendence and immanence, order and spontaneity, commissioning a nave altar that is a work of art in itself, arranging chairs in an inclusive way, varying the arrangement of the chairs depending on the focus of the occasion (especially Maundy

Thursday, Good Friday, the Easter Dawn Vigil and Pentecost), reducing clutter to include only the furniture required, placing a lectern at the back of the nave for the intercessor, keeping liturgical movement to its bare essentials, and deciding which object will represent God's presence at any one time – cross, Trinity icon or paschal candle – and using lighting to enhance the mood of the occasion.

3 The people of God, in different roles together – reading, praying, preaching, administering Communion, working towards the intentional combination of laity, clergy, all ages, the weaving in of Godly Play occasionally as the preaching of the word for everyone, being clear who is presiding but always as a demonstration of our conviction of the significance of each person, administering Communion to visitors and to young ones who have undertaken simple instruction, and sharing the sacrament first with the infirm, then with the congregation and last among the lay and clergy liturgical ministers.

4 The music – the decision to regard music ministries as equivalent to other ministries in the congregation, interweaving with others and involving as many people as possible, moving away from a robed choir sitting in stalls to an informal music group with a core membership enhanced at various times and seasons, searching for hymns and music that open up the whole person to the Spirit of God.

5 Connecting with the whole of life – deliberately through preaching and invitation sometimes to focus on different vocations such as parenting, medicine or education, links with ecumenical approaches to Justice and Peace, wheeling patients from the wards to worship in hospital, action against poverty, Street Pastors, the People's Kitchen and the local food pantry.

6 In courses of learning, encourage those just beginning to be presented to the congregation for their interest and prayer, and similarly at the end; and if there are exhibitions or photographs or banners, let them be part of the liturgy.

7 Embodying the entire work of the church – deliberately including in the liturgy the giving of bishop's permissions to administer Communion, welcoming and saying goodbye to community members, fund-raising and social events, reflecting on a pilgrimage and interviews of visitors from other parts of the world Church.

8 The presider works closely with whichever team member is acting as deacon, articulates the theme of the readings, ensures that newcomers are welcomed, that life stages are celebrated, that the young ones light the altar candles and are prayed with by the deacon as part of the opening greeting, that there is a shape to the liturgy and its contents are proportional to each other in length. He or she acts as a point of stability while others move around, holds the community to silent reflection and gives confidence.

If those are habits adopted by some churches, what would be appropriate in yours and how would they be spoken of and worked towards?

The hospitality of God

Every Christian age has produced its pioneers who have lived on the frontiers, recalling people to what has been lost, opening themselves again to the Holy Spirit, discovering new practices, reforming old ones, discerning what of the past to keep and what to reject. The sections in Christian libraries marked 'spirituality' are testimony to the intense search of the past 100 years for growing in the spirit and growing in personal maturity. The emphasis in more recent times has turned again to communal spirituality that carries resonance with the desert fathers and mothers, the Celtic minsters and the monastic round of Scripture, work, praise and community tasks. At the Reformation the hope was that parish churches would fill the gap by providing a forum for intense experiences of corporate prayer, worship and pastoral care.

Graham Cray and others (2010) have explored how the ancient monastic tradition of fleeing centres of power and creating alternative communities could be relived in completely different environments today. Their report on the New Monasticism describes the texture and comments on many experiments and networks of companions. Seeking to share in the resurrection life made possible through the Spirit, they testify to glimpses of intense contact with the Trinity leading to extensity in evangelism and sharing in God's work for the salvation of people and the whole of Creation. The Rutba House community has distilled 12 marks of a New Monasticism as an ecumenical and prophetic witness (2005, and see <www.newmonasticism.org>).

These marks embrace a range of ways of subverting dominating forms of power, through radical sharing of resources, hospitality, social justice, mutual obedience, formation in Christ, intentional community life, allowing for people of all ages, married and celibate, a shared rule of life, ecological awareness, concern for peace and dedication to prayer. There are links with MacIntyre's sense of humanity being at a turning point requiring local forms of community to sustain intellectual and moral life (2007, p. 263). The New Monasticism longs for the unity of all things in Christ, seeking virtues, habits and grace that can move humanity beyond accepting things as they are:

> Currently the greatest joy . . . is engaging with six young interns who are pressing me to learn and share all I can about discipleship, community and service. Our core curriculum has been the Gospel of Luke as we examine how Jesus engaged with disciples to form them in the Messianic community. What I'm writing here reflects an ardent hope the Holy Spirit is giving us that God is forming many young people for a new generation of prophetic Christian community. (David Janzen 2005, p. 82)

Surveying a wide spectrum of emerging churches, Mary Gray-Reeves and Michael Perham ask, 'What is the Spirit saying to the churches?' (2011, pp. 133ff.). Among their findings they include awareness of:

- emergent churches that consist of perhaps ten to twelve people and are not aiming to grow any larger or move to a larger building;
- others with up to 150 people;
- an emphasis on intimacy and a high degree of participation;
- new churches existing alongside, not replacing, 'inherited' churches – but having an influence in the way of previous movements of the Spirit;
- emergent churches dealing with the pain of those excluded from traditional churches – for reasons of gender, sexual orientation, behaviour or theology;
- people of different views belonging to the same community – not necessarily agreeing but able to handle difference;
- communities built on relationships that intentionally foster intimacy, vulnerability and acceptance;

- prayerful engagement with Scripture and life as a key part of worship.

Their inspiring report on what they have observed contains six insights of conditions when worship can draw contemporary people to Christ:

1 Baptism and Eucharist: where belonging, behaving and believing occur in different ways for different people; showing that God is 'hospitable' leads to an emphasis on welcome, open table, the invitation to a lifetime of journeying with Jesus, exploring faith, care for the worried and confused, delighting in noisy toddlers, greeting newcomers at coffee, all mirroring the hospitality of Godself. They observe the benefits of not protecting the altar from the non-confirmed while recognizing that this will be divisive. They comment that John's Gospel puts the feeding of the 5,000 at the start of the evangelist's teaching that Jesus is the bread of life. And they also recognize that the accounts of the Last Supper are exclusive – they don't mention the women at all.

2 Liturgical planning and preparation: when this is shared by many and the expectation is of wide participation and 'ownership', rather than just turning up to a service, there is an intensifying of experience. Also it seems likely that working in a team to plan liturgy can enlarge faith and lives possibly more than coming to the worship itself. They comment that this is greedy of time and sometimes a simple 'provided' service is what's possible. Suppose that 25 per cent of the congregation in one month have an involvement in the planning and this is rotated – consider the potential impact on their growth.

3 Open space: sometimes instead of a single preacher after a Scripture reading, group exploration of faith and life can take place at 'stations'. These are not fixed groups, so you move on if you're not connecting with a particular leader or discussion. Such conversations lead into prayer so there is a wholeness in the liturgy. They comment wisely how easy it would be for an individual to avoid hearing what he or she wishes to avoid, though in a mature community this is not insurmountable.

4 Enjoying complexity rather than trying to make mystery

over-simple: the report notices the importance of there being many-layered occasions, designed for diverse people, to prevent the situation where only a few kinds of people are being nurtured and therefore present. Tactile ways of praying include icons, prayer beads, candles and other artefacts, treasuring what is old as well as new (Matthew 13.52). A rich feast includes all kinds of music, traditional and contemporary, pilgrimage, fasting, penitence and celebration. The motto seems to be 'bring out something old and give it a try'.

5 'The New Monasticism': when conventional religious life is waning, fresh expressions of community flourish. To draw on old monastic wisdom, recapitulated, is to provide stability for individuals and the emerging church movement.

6 Essentially occupy the space we are in but with renewed confidence. There are things that need to change, but look for the Holy Spirit to pitch his tent among us and show us how to celebrate the liturgy, be open to Scripture, to one another and to the world, to experience the love, beauty and holiness of God, to be more adventurous, in a mixed economy of traditional and new.

I believe any parish staff team – with others locally – could benefit from studying *The Hospitality of God* (Gray-Reeves and Perham 2011) and recognize an opportunity to work to some of its virtues and habits. Many Anglican parishes, formed by the Parish Communion Movement, have a strong tradition of over half a century of a Sung Eucharist being the central act of worship around which most of the existing people gather.

In our parish we had been searching for a way to connect with families that had brought infants for baptism and parents and members of the uniformed organizations. Sharing conversation on hospitality alerted us to make it a new priority of time and resource to offer something for everyone – reworking 'Stir-Up Sunday' at the start of Advent, carol services both 'traditional' and creative, including skyping other churches as part of the worship, the development of a contemplative space, Christingle and conversation around issues about simpler celebrations of Christmas created by the current economic crisis. This led us to want to offer a space for families to do something together for Christmas and offer an 'alternative' vision of what Christmas is about. It was a lot about meeting people where they were – that is, doing Christmas in Advent, offering home-made alternatives to bought presents and having fun as a family making them, an Advent calendar for adults challenging the usual frenetic rush, and worship that did in fact have an Advent theme.

The Hospitality of God survey offers impetus to set up a group that could mobilize a good number of adults to offer two-hour Sunday afternoon 'services' that combine invitation, welcome, versatile use of the interior of the church, things both separate and together for parents and children, food and a short act of worship that sums up the afternoon. The fact that it worked as well as it did in our church came as a surprise, and what we learnt was not only that we were able to offer something attractive to others, but that those who took part in preparing and delivering the first one grew too – it was fun for us to do something together as a parish and in the end we were just being who we were as Church.

Since then we have learnt more about the need to make sure the planning group moves on (from valuable and fascinating conversations for themselves) to detailed planning and distribution of tasks, to advertise and communicate more effectively, to make it clear why we're engaging people in craft activities – how they relate to the theme – and to ensure we don't accidentally patronize people. Also we've experimented in giving a space for the parents on their own for a while, inviting them, for example, to consider what it was they appreciated from their own parents and what they would most want to hand on to their own children now. On the whole, though, we find that parents prefer to shelter behind their children until they find their feet in church.

This enterprise, costly in time and energy, seems to work because it is appropriate to our context and time. There is no blueprint to be followed carefully, although there are routine questions to be asked and followed up in planning each event. It's definitely not a formula; it did not grow out of a committee trying to set up a new 'service'; it evolved and continues to evolve, and will definitely go on changing again, depending on who is participating, and will adapt to our own shifting circumstances. The next stage is to persuade the church council that this is no longer an experiment. It must happen more often and with a budget and, with the commitment of the church council and congregation, become as significant as our Sunday morning Eucharists.

Learning from the New Monasticism

When churches begin to emphasize intense engagement with God, the burning bush, the living presence of God, encounter, a borehole into the divine fire are images that quickly come into awareness.

The history of monastic communities seems to display the virtues of exploring, dissatisfaction, diving deeper into God, being limitless, rebellious, courageous in starting again, tough-minded, rhythmical, accepting being loved by God along with all Creation, characterized by joy and freedom. How would we build habits of church community now that are identified with some of the monastic virtues of previous eras, clear but open, respecting the past but led today by the Holy Spirit's new call?

Within a long and varied tradition of monastic life, the Rule of Benedict (early sixth century) was written for a group who had chosen to live together to focus on prayer in a community rhythm ordered towards the search for God. The Rule's 75 short chapters were a product of Benedict's own community experience and a collation of inherited wisdom. It has a vision worked out through detailed regulations about lifestyle: clothing, food, sleep and work–rest balance. By the ninth century the Rule was a key influence in religious life and continues to be a significant and flexible partner in the conversation about intensity of relating with God and God's work among all people. The Rule with its practices indicates the enduring potential of the lived-out virtues of Christian community.

A great deal of wisdom concerning the potential for living the Rule of Benedict and its many adaptions in religious and secular life today is mapped out in *Doing Business with Benedict* (Kit Dollard *et al.* 2002). Abbott Timothy Wright, OSB, summarizes the notion of attraction that can lead us into a brief set of suggestions about how ordinary local churches could discern its value for their own living of a virtue ecclesiology:

> One of the amazing things about a monastic community is the diversity of personalities found within it: the larger the community, the greater the spread. People don't join monasteries because they like the monk they met in the guesthouse, nor do they join simply because they find the Abbott a sympathetic character. People are attracted to the monastic life because the

overall aim of that life is inherently attractive: it is answering a need deep inside their hearts . . . they have fallen in love with God who touches them. Each monastery will deliver the dream in different ways and as in all forms of human life, this will be both fulfilling and frustrating.

(Wright in Dollard *et al.* 2002, p. 37)

Equally, Franciscan houses with their open combination of action and contemplation, sacraments and openness to every aspect of our poverty, could be touchstones for imaging a richer parish church life. The ordered spontaneity of friary worship and living point to a different way of seeing the whole of life, ecumenical, inclusive, taking many forms, always reforming, sitting light to traditions from the past and being pillars of fire for the present moment.

Seven habits of local churches acting as religious houses

David Ford describes how a eucharistic self, through apprenticeship to Christian disciplines, is blessed, placed, timed and commanded through a 'wisdom of habituation' that is embodied in liturgical practices:

Repetition after repetition of hearing scripture and its interpretation, of repentance, of intercession and petition, of the kiss of peace, of communion, of praising and thanking, all within a dramatic pattern that slowly becomes second nature: who can tell in advance what sort of self is being shaped year after year as these practices are interwoven thoughtfully with all the rest of life? (Ford 1999, pp. 164f.)

If we lay aside all our historical prejudices about the religious life together with all idealized portraits, we could imagine how the virtues, for example, of praise, hospitality, forgiveness, humility, integrity, life–work balance, life-long learning and inner conversion might be scaled across from monastic life to the practices of any Christian community that intends to walk with Jesus. Walking with Jesus, as all disciples have known, brings its share of anguish and hostility as we choose to let go of group securities and allow ourselves to be healed and transformed (John 12.42–43).

With so many to consider, here are just seven ideas of communal practices evolving from monastic living that could be endlessly developed in a more loosely affiliated Christian chaplaincy or parish:

1 *Worshipping and praying* Agreeing and planning ways of worshipping and praying that grow the community towards its virtues and final purpose, radically making these practices central to the community's life, reshaping architecture and the arrangement of furniture to match the liturgy, being open to radical diversity with one community or group of churches, networking with practices across a wide field, noticing which images of God are included and which are absent, regularly reviewing the practice and the benefits to participants.

2 *Recognizing gifts of the Spirit* Valuing different gifts and skills, finding resources to coach and develop personal gifts, encouraging people to delight in who they are and what they do, ensuring that no one is overburdened and that the community receives only those gifts that seem appropriate at the present moment and that careful time and responsibility markers are laid down and regularly revised.

3 *Encouraging innovators* Noticing who likes change, functions well at the beginning of a new project and can initiate and facilitate innovation in a team, ensuring that innovations have sufficient resources, keeping innovators in touch with those responsible for inherited patterns of working, ensuring that innovators have the chance to network with others elsewhere and monitoring progress, and being aware of when innovation might lead to frustration and separation from the community.

4 *Energetically greeting the newcomer* Offering a warm welcome and courtesy to guests, new arrivals and strangers, expecting demands to be made on the community that may be alarming or time-consuming, presenting the stranger with opportunity for conversations, not being shocked by strangers' narratives, expecting some guests to stay while others move on, being prepared to give an account to the new arrival of the virtues and practices of the community and being cautious about expecting anything in return or involvement in practices.

5 *Belonging in maturity* Accepting that at different stages of life people will 'belong' in a wide variety of ways, inviting and forming

adult–adult behaviour, having the means of correcting fractures in community life, valuing material objects as signs of God's presence, inviting everyone to notice the effect of their ways of participating, keeping house rules, expecting cooperation by actively keeping in touch with others and the leaders, being generous in praising, thanking and supporting one another, responsibly critiquing the community and offering to be part of necessary changes, and being an advocate for the community.

6 *Living the virtues* Participating by helping to make the community happen or work, taking responsibility for thinking and acting for excellence in the practices of the community, being an agent of reconciliation, noticing mistakes and creatively challenging, taking part in worship and public gatherings, following personal disciplines of prayer, learning and lifestyle that flow from the virtues of the community, showing compassion to others and meeting their needs, being vulnerable and allowing the community to serve us, and keeping in day-to-day contact with others, face to face or through electronic networks.

7 *Seeking the good of the neighbourhood* Actively seeking to be part of a place, acknowledging the contribution to the locality of community members, being consciously ecological in practice, stewarding land, caring for any in difficulty, working for good relationships with neighbours, adding to the store of goodness in a place, and keeping abreast of and discerning when to intervene in economic and political issues, being aware of the community's vested interest, taking stock of its contribution to the wider community through ownership and maintenance of property and pay and conditions of anyone employed by the community.

Worship and spirituality core group

Context determines the habits and possibilities of local churches in making decisions about worship and nurturing spiritual development in the community. My own recent experience as parish priest has included leading a small core group that prays and talks possibilities for both routine and developmental forms of corporate worship and prayer. I offer this in the spirit of 'scaling across' and invite readers to consider how or whether this could be valuable in their own churches.

When this worship group has outlined suggestions, for example about Advent or Holy Week, a liturgy planning group of those involved in presenting worship meets to plan the detail and possibly have second thoughts on the plan. This is not so simple because worship is the key to all we are and do as Church, yet everyone has strong views; few people like long meetings and yet no one is content simply to implement what others have suggested without comment. The effectiveness of that meeting requires everyone to be aware of contributing towards a balance between covering the whole agenda in two and half hours and giving everyone the chance to contribute, as well as simply not repeating the initial work of the core group.

Similarly, a musicians' group, meeting in the regular rhythm of the core group and the planning group, will then explore what will be needed from the organ and who to approach for something more creative, such as brass for the Easter Vigil or a solo guitarist for a family worship event. While we are fully aware of our limitations, Table 10.1 overleaf outlines the core group's aims presented to the church council for 2011–12 as part of our Mission Action Plan.

What matters most in this is the virtue of moving beyond the mere survival of a particular church towards feeding the faith of everyone present and of those who are so much in need but not yet present. Across a group of churches – or in one large one – how can we develop a wider spectrum of ways of worshipping and of participation? How can we move from being churches where people come, look and listen to shared speaking, singing, action and movement? Priests and people together carry the privilege, within our resources, of celebrating all the faces of God through words, music and opportunities to attract others. There's no need for this to be overwhelming, even though aiming for excellence in practice is greedy of time and the energy of leaders has to be constantly reviewed.

The role of the priest and ministry team is to mediate between the existing worshippers and those who are searching for a place in the community. This means recognizing the experience and particular learning of clergy, Readers and others who have followed scriptural or spiritual disciplines, but also listening intently to and being freely accountable to the worshippers. Through persuasion and teaching and an insistence on serious rigour being applied to public worship, *episkope* can be exercised by the parish team, hopefully in positive and creative liaison with the bishop and diocesan team.

Table 10.1 Our aims for 2011–12

Theme: Worship and spirituality
Vision: To help the congregation grow in intimacy with God
Who: Coordinator; administrator; music coordinator; sacristan

Actions	Timescale	Planned outcome
Nurture the liturgy planning group's work to maintain the regular pattern of worship on Sundays, festivals and weekdays	Continuing	Foster deeper personal relationship with God within the context of a community of mutual care as a sign of God's kingdom
Continue with others to explore how the whole community – all ages, temperaments, stages of faith development – are included, become participants and are offered opportunities for transformation	Continuing	Make worship accessible to all in the parish, and something in which all can participate and be fed and challenged Continued delivery of Lent, Advent and study groups by the laity Make connections with daily life and discipleship
Explore how worship can be a vital element in the 100 years celebrations, e.g. the provision of a Eucharist to mark the laying of the foundation stone and a deanery service	Planning prior to May 2011	By giving thanks for what has been, helping the community to look forward to where God may be leading us
Explore creative use of worship space as redevelopment takes place	Continuing during redevelopment and beyond	Assist community in recognizing that redevelopment reflects something of what we are trying to embody as a community
Assist the congregation to develop patterns of musical expression that serve the above	Congregational meeting planned for end of October 2010	Encourage participation of all

Table 10.1 (continued)

Actions	Timescale	Planned outcome
Foster existing spiritual pathways and support new developments, e.g. in contemplative prayer	Evening Prayer format being 'trialled' for meetings Possible contemplative prayer twice a month	Helping people deepen their prayer life and accept the consequences that flow from that
Year of Spiritual Pilgrimage	To coincide with 100 year anniversary of Christian worship on site of St Mary's	To ensure connections with God are included in social and fun-raising events

11

Open and pastoral

Church as the giving and receiving of love

Compassion invites you to aspire to an awakened heart, to trust in its value and be committed to its realization. To hold in your heart and mind the resolve to bring an end to suffering, wherever you meet it, is a transforming motivation that allows you to step out of arguing, blaming, avoiding and the ceaseless efforts to fix the world. (Christina Feldman 2005, p. 48)

Pastoral care in the image of God: the common work of God's people

Bringing together action and enquiry invites reflection on the caring activities of God and human communities.

The timbre of the 'pastoral care' must intentionally hold in balance the Christian ministry of showing concern for the sick and the distressed while moving away from the one-way emphasis embodied in phrases like 'I have ten parishes to care for' or the single focused expectation of a congregation that the leaders are principally there to look after them.

When we explore pastoral care in the light of the walking and healing of Jesus, the central notion is that of liberation or the intense yet courteous invitation to be transformed. Jesus invites the man by the pool at Siloam to decide on his destiny just as he asks others, 'What do you want from me?' Jesus revealed God as one who can be trusted, who above all invites us into intimate relationship, as one who cannot be known all at once but gradually as the Spirit leads, in story and experience as much as in defining language, as vulnerable and available among the poorest, as known in another human being, often enigmatically, and together in mutual service and friendship. Pastoral ministry can be seen in this light as a way of helping people over time, in community, to find confidence, meaning and purpose in their lives where God is the deepest source.

Pastoral care as a communal craft

Society generally now has few expectations of Christian pastoral care but the residual memory is of clergy visits. A lay member of the church offering pastoral care can still disappoint even committed members of the congregation, until hopefully it is experienced as nurturing, generous and not hurried. The classical-clerical way of pastoral care is still very much the norm, and for many clergy is a key way of using their gifts and identifying their priestly task as clinical-pastoral. We need to be aware, though, that it can make us think of God as one alone and 'care' as essentially a one-way activity provided by professionals.

More consistent with the theology we are espousing here is a reaction against the clerical paradigm towards a communal or relational practice of pastoral care. In this approach the same person at different times will be the minister and the one ministered to. Pastoral theologian Karen Scheib has identified four interconnected virtues of a community that mediates rather than provides pastoral care:

1 Relationality and community are central.
2 Human development is a relational process which occurs within a social context.
3 Individual differences and cultural diversity are highly valued.
4 Mutuality and reciprocity are the hallmarks of the practices of pastoral care.   (Scheib in Lartey 2006, p. 124)

So, for example, in helping a family plan a funeral the following ways of involving everyone concerned militate against simply having a minister take the funeral:

- The aim is both to honour the dead and to allow the bereaved to grieve and care for one another.
- The family may need positive encouragement to use the church building rather than the crematorium.

- Readings are negotiated.
- The family or someone who knew the deceased well prepares and perhaps also speaks a tribute.
- The preaching of the gospel will be apposite.
- CDs may be included, or a poem.
- Secular songs as well as hymns may be sung.
- A large photograph of the deceased and a candle may stand near the coffin.
- At the farewell, members of the family may stand with the priest, around and possibly touching the coffin, or may place a precious or beautiful object on it.

As Lartey summarizes,

> the whole tapestry of the liturgical event is woven around the stuff of the person's life as it interacts with our common life story. In all of this, sight is not lost of the bereaved community and connections are made to enable them to grieve and then gently move on. A funeral service, when handled carefully, is an instance of . . . expressive pastoral theology.   (2006, pp. 16f.)

Welcoming, integrating and caring

Pastoral care as performance of good news could be likened to artistic performance, uncovering and communicating our experience of God among us. The question is how a church council could work to create a welcoming, integrating and caring group that doesn't deny the value of face-to-face conversations between laity and clergy, especially when someone is facing terminal illness. So the purpose would be to create an environment where newcomers, visitors and regular worshippers feel equally welcome and valued and to provide opportunities and encouragement for people to grow in the love of God and one another. The practices might be to:

- define the role of 'welcomers', ensuring all ages are included;
- identify newcomers and encourage them to join the church community;
- increase awareness about those who may be absent or have specific

needs, and take appropriate action;

- encourage all comers to participate actively in church life;
- encourage older men, as well as women, to have the confidence to get to know, encourage and watch out for younger ones facing contemporary pressures and opportunities;
- coordinate the pastoral care network;
- establish a referral system that meets emergency, interim and long-term needs;
- set up and maintain an accurate record of everyone who has contact;
- look into ways of providing information at the end of services to encourage people to return.

To form congregations in the wisdom needed to be centred on God in community, against a backdrop of a society of very different values, is a vital agenda. Given the pressure on churches and church members from all directions, this must happen through habits that are organic, mutual, gender-inclusive, intergenerational and hospitable:

> If our thought and practice are to be inclusive, they need to be debated by a great variety of different groups; they can never be set up as new dogmas. This is a continuing challenge for us, because the temptation to be 'in the right' is a danger that can be found in all of us.   (Gebara 1999, p. 14)

Alternative styles of thinking and action are emerging but need to be highlighted and encouraged as deliberate and habitual through:

- teaching and preaching, passing on to new generations the new life in Christ;
- the example of those who are already seeking their own spiritual growth and that of others;
- allowing ourselves to be open to being 'spoken to' by other members in the congregation;
- walking with those who are ill or physically limited for a short or long period;
- assuming that this building up of people is more than 'women's work' – so, in Richard Rohr's terms, how older men can watch

out for the younger ones in all their contemporary pressures and opportunities;

- everyone noticing how they are contributing to the quality of relationships in the church;
- sharing in the responsibility of desiring and building a grown-up Church where everyone is regarded with dignity and invited to adult–adult relating;
- attempting to live the wisdom we most admire;
- the exchange of the 'gifts' of experience, life learning, insight and resilience;
- offering new perspectives to one another through conversation and more formally convened house groups;
- being individually part of a community of trust and confidentiality – recovering something of a 'village' consciousness;
- watching out for and offering sustained commitment to the vulnerable or single adult who could easily feel ostracized or for the child of a family with a single parent;
- finding ways to challenge one another as well as support, for each person's own development and for the welfare of the church community and neighbourhood.

Open to the neighbourhood

At the close of the Eucharist we are told to 'go'. Wells links the sharing of gifts in worship and Christian community with practical action in the world, 'a reordering of society and a reassembly of creation' (2006, p. 193). The Durham Receptive Ecumenism project found clear evidence of this connection in most denominations. It may be that it was more important than the direct occurrences of 'social (care, concern, action)' and that respondents may have felt that the practice of service to the world was incorporated within 'mission' (although this was unclear in most respondents' answers). Similar words or phrases revealed that there were exceptions:

> the main elements of our faith are worship, mission, both in terms of . . . all the elements of social action and also evangelism, the whole realm of mission. (Baptist)

A belief that we are all working towards the kingdom of God would be the phrase that you would use, which I understand as working towards . . . ourselves and the people around us and the world being as God intended it to be.   (Anglican)

I am relating Alasdair MacIntyre's theories about the pursuit of excellence and good judgement in practices chosen specifically to help an institution achieve its end (*telos*) to the practices of Church, locally and regionally. The term 'virtue' is employed not in terms of norms, rights and moral theory, though gospel communities will always want to be struggling to know how to act ethically in a relativist culture. By 'practice' I mean complex and developing forms of cooperative social activity by which we come to excel in the virtues. It would be difficult to imagine practices for building up social life that were in themselves injurious or degrading. (MacIntyre seems here to elevate white-collar jobs over working-class jobs.) Church as a network of communion is attuned for learning to recognize and learn from those individuals and communities who have discovered practices that foster hopeful and liberating virtues.

Moore is appreciative of Wells' framework of practices (see page 72), which he adapts, recognizing that Wells is not using language in quite the same way as MacIntyre.

In adapting the academic discourse on what might be called practices or sub-practices, my own intuition and experience is that the notion of a small number of practices to serve a 'virtuous' church's final purpose has potential for releasing new energy in re-imagining Church. However, we are in danger of returning to a blueprint mentality unless we recognize how context requires that proposals be adapted and categorized, worked out through a varying range of language, habits and practices of varying complexity.

One practice in particular emerged in the Receptive Ecumenism research that was not explicit in Wells' work. This was in the area of personal relationship (often expressed in terms of 'loving relationship') with God. Some saw this as a practice in its own right. Some associated this practice with a sense of calling or vocation to a Christian practice, for example loving others:

The main elements of my faith are that God loves me and every single member of the human race without condition . . . God inviting us to work with him to make the world the sort of place he wants it to be. (Anglican)

And within that relationship (with God and others) I invoke a particular vocation as priest that's very important to me too. To maintain that is a privilege. But also I think that it's a joyful thing to do and enjoyable too. Wears me out sometimes [*both laugh*] but it's enjoyable. (Roman Catholic)

I am somebody who firmly believes that part of our calling is to be always prepared to work for the social good, so I work with a training minister in a new location, in providing support for asylum seekers to provide housing. (Methodist)

Reflection on a local church cooperating with traders at a shopping centre for the benefit of the neighbourhood

The local shopping centre is a rather faded 1960s shopping development towards the edge of a seaside parish. Several years of neglect by a landlord has meant that the shop fronts, the surfaces and the general feel of the area make it seem unloved and unlovely. However, if you scratch the surface you discover that, beyond first sight, this is a vibrant shopping centre with all but two of the twenty or so shopping units full. The shops – a café, baker, post office, hairdresser, barber, newsagent, estate agent, alteration shop, funeral director and several take-aways, among others – provide a hub for the neighbourhood. In addition, the opening of a Tesco Metro and a soft-play has made the centre a place that people regularly visit during the day and the night. Here an Anglican priest, my colleague Benjamin Carter, expresses his own experience:

In a densely populated suburban parish with few shared areas of public space, I began to recognize that, despite its looks, here was a crucial meeting place, a place where God is clearly at work. Taking this view, in conjunction with the Baptist minister whose congregation meet in the local First School, a series of meetings were organized with the shopkeepers to see what could be done together. The approach that emerged was to both be clearly from the church (I always wear a dog-collar) but be clear that our starting point as churches are as groups 'always passionate about the communities in which they serve'.

As mentioned above there was a history of poor management by the landlord, who then became insolvent. Previous attempts to meet as a group of shopkeepers had foundered on the impossibility of getting any movement or change from the landlord. Understanding this historic position at our first meeting, held in the coffee shop, we offered a simple process of Appreciative Inquiry to focus not on what we might change, but on what worked and what we could build on.

The new 'presence' to one another meant that the upshot of that first meeting, at which about half of the shops were represented, was an interest in organizing some community events in the centre as a way of attracting people to the shops (from the businesses' point of view) and providing a shared space for community activity from the point of view of the churches. From this meeting two main actions happened. The first was that we began to organize a series of events for Christmas. The second was that, separate from our meeting, contact was made by the local council with the shopkeepers. From this second link, and because we had ourselves already made steps towards building community events in the centre, money was made available by the council to provide a 20-foot Christmas tree, together with all the infrastructure. With this in place we organized a 'tree-lighting' with children from the First School singing carols, which brought about 200 people to an open-air event. At this I was able to say a prayer, which all responded to and respected.

In addition to this event the funeral directors paid for fliers to advertise additional Christmas events in the centre – most notably the school Christmas Fayre and carol singing on the Saturday before Christmas. The reverse of the flier also provided the times and places for the Christmas services at the four local churches (Anglican, Baptist, Methodist and Roman Catholic). At this latter event the funeral directors also provided for a Santa to visit on a sleigh, with gifts for the children and face painting. In all about 150 children and their families were served by this event. The carols were sung by members of the four local churches, and St Mary's also used the occasion to give away a Christmas tree decoration which included our Christmas service dates.

Following the success of the Christmas events, plans were put in place in the new year to build on this with a summer event. The Queen's Diamond Jubilee was seen as the best event to focus on. The planning group – which involved four shop-keepers, a representative from Rotary, the council community engagement officer, the Baptist minister and myself – met regularly to organize a simple event.

It is hard to identify what it was that worked about that event, but two themes came to the fore from the Jubilee party which have imbued this project, and continue to do so. The first is that the organization of it from the start was not about putting on successful events but providing a forum and space through which events happen. This means that, while being organized, we have not been goal-driven, preferring to do something well and letting others join in with what they can bring and offer to this. For example, the funeral directors brought the Santa to the Christmas events, and before the planning meeting was held the face painter offered to come to the Jubilee party.

The second theme is that of hospitality. It has been vital that these events have been free at the point of access. This has meant that all have been welcome. Worth, identity and enjoyment cannot be marked by how much one can spend, or on what. The hospitality has been to provide time and space to be with one another in a community and middle-class culture where they are often in short supply. At the Jubilee party it was interesting to hear people saying they were able just to stay and talk to people without the constant nagging of children for more money for this or that.

Both these themes reflect back on the culture and identity of St Mary's as a church where we try to be both open and available to the community whose church it is, and also offer a way of being in and viewing the world which does confirm expectations of the world around us. So at the Jubilee party everything was free. It was enough that people felt welcome. This was also evident when one of the staff team was approached by a gruff man during the carol singing who asked, 'So what are you collecting for?' The staff member replied, 'Nothing, but do have a free Christmas decoration from us, and Happy Christmas!'

Looking to the future we are planning similar Christmas events which will this year involve a fund-raising evening in St Mary's Church, which the shopkeepers wanted to use as their church. Added to that are further plans for a summer fayre. There is now a need to develop a team of people willing to maintain and grow this link into the centre, to continue to support the shopkeepers and to further the community engagement and identity which this work has created.

Above all this work has provided a very subtle and perhaps almost imperceptible change in the identity of the church. In middle-class seaside suburbs church could be, and perhaps has been, viewed as the capstone of a respectable life, the Tory Party at prayer. This work has hopefully helped the community see a church which is less interested in people being 'good', but rather meets them where they are and seeks to walk with them wherever they are going. There have been two consequences from this subtle evangelism of a different image of God. First, members of the community have been able to find out what it is to be a Christian and a follower of Christ in a world where church membership is not synonymous or necessary for those wishing to look respectable. The Church is about being God's people in that place, showing signs and ways to the world as God would have it.

Second, this work has helped communicate clearly and gently to the community as a whole that St Mary's is a group of people passionate about the community in which it is based. But more than that, it has helped suggest to people that this passion is not drawn just from a community spirit. It has its roots in something deeper and more glorious: a God who is already at work where people are inviting us all to join in.

Christian coffee shops that are lay-led are increasing in number. The struggles of being a Christian in everyday life can be explored here, where God is not confined to a Holy Club in which going to church has almost become a hobby.

For churches to be open and mutually caring deliberately as a sign of the kingdom is to be a pointer to a different kind of society and world community. Another church described the persistence of an open and trusting discussion group that eventually led to the erosion of a culture in the congregation that could only be described as the 'tyranny of the elderly', whose desire was to keep church 'formal and polite'. In this group, where confidentiality and honesty were paramount, it was 'all right to say anything, all right to say it tough, and all right to find it difficult now. It's now allowed to say someone is wrong and God is in the conversation.' It requires such determined energy to become a church of real exchange in which all can feel welcome. A Lutheran community in Manhattan is proud of the sign over its door, 'An especial welcome to gay and lesbian couples'.

To care deeply, authentically and theologically in this world today requires an extensive vision, passion and contemplative action. Churches can contribute to a vision and practices of a healthier world community through intentionally being agents of transformation precisely where we are. This requires a knowledge that is beyond information, respectful engagement across a kaleidoscope of differences to begin to mediate the wisdom of God in watching out for the world.

12

Communicating

Letting down barriers and being real

A community that turns to one another creates a spirit of welcome for all its members. It relies on the fact that people want to be engaged, that they want to learn and contribute to their community. It recognizes that people will step forward as leaders when they discover an issue they care about. It pays attention to the web of relations, and works to include not exclude. It keeps inviting in more people for their rich diversity of ideas, heritage, perspectives. As it does all this, a miraculous gift reveals itself. It doesn't matter if no one is coming to help. We have all we need, right here, right now, among us all.

(Margaret Wheatley in Wheatley and Frieze 2011, p. 225)

Church 'as one of another'

Collaborative working demands an inner personal security, respect for others, a willingness to restrain ourselves to be part of a whole and the practice of self-awareness. In the parish where I have been vicar for over seven years we have established regular ways of reflecting on the purpose and experience of the various ministries of the congregation and ordained and Readers. This happens within my regular review meetings with each of the staff team and with others holding significant responsibilities. In the more formally structured regular conversations with those who are canonically ordered we have developed a light framework to guide us each time:

1 Agreed actions from the last supervision meeting.
2 What have you done/learnt in the last few weeks – personally, in your role and about the church and its work in the neighbourhood?
3 How has your experience been different from your expectations?

4 Are there issues in the working relationship that need addressing?
5 Other issues to discuss.
6 What are you discerning as your role here at the moment?

Through regular conversation of an Appreciative Inquiry style, our staff team of laity and clergy has identified practices by which to test our work and offer mutual encouragement:

1 a corporate and consistent presentation of ourselves as a team in the church;
2 a clear, intimate and honest approach to our inner team life;
3 effective communication and information sharing within and from the team;
4 regular prayer for one another, mutual caring and a desire for 'presence';
5 mutual respect;
6 sharing and supporting one another in keeping the practices in our personal rule of life.

That's not to say we don't have our differences and the need sometimes for tough conversations with one another, for example when someone sabotages the virtues and habits by which we work. When a team member speaks without care or lacks self-awareness or simply pushes for a personal preference rather than helping discern what's best for the parish, that person undermines effective leadership towards change. In the spirit of a relational and adult practice of church, resorting to reprimanding or scapegoating a team member in response to his or her actions is inappropriate.

Gil Rendle, through the Alban Institute's regular blog, suggests the development of a 'covenant of leadership' to uphold within a congregation. This is not in terms of rules that must be kept. Relationships are better kept healthy by covenants, which offer us goals that are in keeping with the values and teaching of Christian faith. Covenants offer ways of discussing the behaviour and practices we have chosen to adopt in our work together as leaders, managing change and celebrating with difference. When developing a covenant of leadership with a group of congregational leaders, Rendle explores recent conflictual experiences and then develops positive statements about healthy and appropriate behaviour around which team members are willing to covenant. The list of covenant behaviours then becomes a written agreement about the practices of the team. The example she offers (see Box 12.1) could be for either the whole congregation or the leadership team. Even in the very different context of a mainline UK church this still has an important resonance.

Box 12.1 A covenant of leadership
Our promises to God
We promise to pray, alone and together, to thank God and to ask for God's help in our lives and in our work for our church, and we promise to listen to God's answer to us.

Our promises to our church family
We promise to demonstrate our leadership and commitment to our church by our example.

We promise to support our church's pastors and staff, so their efforts can be most productive.

We promise to try to discover what is best for our church as a whole, not what might be best for us or for some small group in the church.

Our promises to each other on [the governing board]
We promise to respect and care for each other.

We promise to treat our time on [the board] as an opportunity to make an important gift to our church.

We promise to listen with an open, non-judgemental mind to the words and ideas of the others in our church and on [the board].

We promise to discuss, debate and disagree openly in [board] meetings, expressing ourselves as clearly and honestly as possible, *so* we are certain the [board] understands *our* point of view.

We promise to support the final decision of [the board], whether it reflects our view or not.

Rendle comments,

> this group of leaders wrestled with the specific behaviours and attitudes that were causing them problems in working effectively in their congregation. Their covenantal promises came out of understanding themselves and choosing to practice values and behaviors of their faith that could change their life and work together. Other congregations that have developed covenants of leadership have necessarily developed different lists that speak to their own needs. Each leadership group needs to identify and address the issues and behaviors relevant for them.
>
> (*Alban Weekly* September 2012)

This is not about *enforcing* behaviours but inviting people into mutual practices that can testify to a way of being Church that animates the intentional practice of the gospel in awareness and mutual love. Rendle suggests reading the covenant together in unison at the beginning of a meeting as a way of reinforcing the goals they have accepted in maturity for their working life together.

Being real with one another

It's time for churches to identify themselves in practices of communion *with* and as an intentional communication *of* the Trinity. Two points need to be made. One is about giving and receiving as opposed to being adversarial; the other is about the honesty that is only available through living not from appearances but from our deepest core.

First, we must learn to leave behind the long history of competition between churches. We can only be the one, catholic church together through all our brokenness and difference. To let go of adversarial rivalry we must embrace recent insights of Miroslav Volf and John Zizioulas on inclusion, where difference constitutes rather than damages communion. Inevitably, loyalties to communities and buildings are built up over years, but Jesus asked, 'Who is my mother, and who are my brothers?' (Matthew 12.48) and challenged us to 'let the dead bury their own dead' (Matthew 8.22). If we are secure in the knowledge of God's love for ourselves, and are realistic that all our insights into liturgy, youth work and mission will always be partial, we can gladly receive from others what they too are discovering.

Second, there will be always be a shadow or underbelly in any virtue we espouse. If we do not own our corporate shadow we shall find we are owned by it. If the explorations triggered by this book are to be authentic, we shall have to be grown up enough to recognize how churches and ministers are often missing the target when it comes to lived virtues. And even when we are trying in genuine ways to please God and have something to be proud of, we have a natural tendency to seek to prove ourselves right, to be competitive and to feed our own ambition. So there is brokenness in our best efforts. If we know this openly there can be less room for egotistical pride in our so-called achievements. As we have noticed throughout this study, the only satisfying way is the way of resting in God's peace through meditation, contemplation, praise, worship and trust. I think it's vital to give this discussion some space.

Trappist monks M. Basil Pennington and Thomas Merton, psychoanalyst D. W. Winnicott and spiritual writer Richard Rohr are leading examples of those who have all contributed to our awareness of the 'false self' in people and communities. The concept of the false self is described by D. W. Winnicott in his article entitled 'Ego distortion in terms of true and false self' (1960). Inadequate mothering, suggests Winnicott, can lead to an infant building up a false set of relationships, and finding it difficult in later life to be 'real' (Winnicott 1960, p. 146). In such cases the personality structure of an individual may be built on this false self foundation. Similar ideas have been discussed as 'narcissistic': an unrealistic sense that unless we are brilliant achievers we are utterly shameful. For persons and churches to occupy a 'good enough' middle space requires emotional resilience. When we operate from the position of the false self, typically we experience greater than usual difficulty in connecting to others and forming meaningful relationships. The result is often a feeling of emptiness, as though a huge hollow existed in our centre. A person may even have the impression that he or she is 'not really living' but merely 'sleepwalking through life'. Winnicott also claims that:

[A] particular danger arises out of the not infrequent tie-up between the intellectual approach and the False Self . . . The world may observe academic success of a high degree, and may find it hard to believe in the very real distress of the individual concerned, who feels 'phoney' the more he or she is successful. (1960, p. 144)

Like most other defensive structures, the false self organization is not always unwanted. A certain amount of false self organization is present in everyone and is necessary for survival, but when the false self is dominant, people and communities settle for a merely polite and mannered social attitude (1960, p. 152).

There's so much material for reflection here on how churches and their representatives see and project themselves, how we manage ourselves in ancient and costly buildings, how we live with uncertainty as public preachers, how we manage our personal needs within community, how we review the work we do and so on. Richard Rohr has contributed an immense amount to the consideration of how ministers and churches can be truly mature. He believes it's the false self in churches that

> settles for ritualism and legalism, and moralism instead of true mysticism (which is available to all once one does not make it a contest or an achievement). The true self is not about requirements, it's about relationship – the quality and capacity for relatedness. This lays the foundation for contemplation. The contemplative does not need to be 'right', but only in relationship. The false self will say its prayers but the true self IS a prayer. This is why Paul can say 'pray always' (Ephesians 6.18). We pray always whenever we live in conscious union with God. Then every action is a prayer no matter how secular, mundane, or ordinary it might appear. (Rohr 2012)

This connects with presencing and self-awareness so that church communities and ministers choose to live from their core or innermost being. Contemplative prayer is the most frequently suggested antidote to being in the grasp of the false self.

Thomas Merton (2003) brings challenging insights into the struggle to find an honest relationship with God and with one another. In considering the false self and the true self, he proposes that 'sin' occurs when people and churches believe they really are the illusory **false self**. This is the person or the church community we truly want to be but which does not exist, because we have not allowed God to bring us into living in his will or love. The true self – person or community – is humbly and intentionally living in the love and mercy of God.

I believe this needs to be emphasized because it is a besetting sin of all church leaders to present ourselves, corporately and personally, as the persons we fancy ourselves to be. If we want to avoid being imposters living behind facades, we need to lay down our defences and come out into God's light.

But in case this makes all hope for church flourishing seem fated, Merton's own story offers a way through. He decided that becoming a famous writer was in fact not God's will but a projection of his own. He eventually realized, having dedicated his life to being a monk, that his skill in writing could be his way of becoming his true self when the seed planted in him by God was **consecrated in order to grow into the source of blessing for others that God intended it to be.** What a great blessing to thousands of people that God was able to bring about that transformation so that wisdom could be shared in Merton's writing.

Practising the virtue of mutual love

This book invites local churches, teams and clergy to ask: 'What are the best questions we can be asking and what conversations will bring agreement on values and habits?' Negative memories of meetings and 'discussions' may immediately make this an unattractive approach. But Appreciative Inquiry methods switch us from competitive 'discussion' (*discutio*) to reflective and inclusive conversations that reflect on creative accounts of moments when churches and teams had important new insights and generative experiences.

Discussion involves a measure of fighting for the right answer and can take us into black holes of what we don't want or what we most fear. Here instead is a pathway that can help Christian communities to identify their ideal future and learn together how to design and implement innovations. This is a confident move away from most ways of operating where we invite a hand-picked group of well-intentioned, articulate people to produce answers and deliver them. Unless we reshape anxiety-producing meetings and ways of working, we continue to exclude and leave speechless many whose contribution is vital.

Ministry as 'one of another'

Critical reflection on the exploration of many forms of 'local shared ministry' across the world reveals the unquestionable need for episcopal and diocesan partnership with local churches in policy and practice. The local ministry movement has given to the Church not a prescriptive set of rules, but a general formula for the shift from an ecclesiology that is predetermined to one constantly reforming through active dialogue between local churches and God's Spirit. Such teams, at their best, are not a substitute for the contribution of the diminishing number of stipendiary clergy, but rather provocative agents and facilitators of human and spiritual development.

We need priests for this new context who can be relaxed facilitators, capable of observing their own part within the interplay of power dynamics, archetypes, politics and emotional exchange. It takes huge courage and skill to bear church conflict. For presiding priests, teams and groups, to keep communities Christian, ordered in love and held in stability is a principal task for those charged with a navigating ministry (Ephesians 6.12). Initial and continuing formation of priests needs to focus on the habits of facilitating dialogue, encouraging the principle of self-organizing, challenging the culture of success, and celebrating the richness and mystery of ambiguity.

A re-invigorated and transformative church emerges as a ministering community rather than as 'volunteers' in tasks delegated from the minister. A challenging test of the priest's aptitude for supporting people in new ministries is when, at the end of a three-year period of carrying a commission, someone can say: 'Thank you, I have grown so much as a person and a Christian through being invited to exercise that ministry.'

Issues about shared or local ministry that concern a diocese include:

- what degree of regulation is desirable;
- how much education and preparation is essential before parishes move to local ministry;
- how any particular church discerns whether local ministry is a helpful initiative;
- what is required of the parish priest for this to flourish;

- what encouragement and resource is necessary from bishop and diocese;
- what form of regular review will be needed;
- how lay energy for their secular vocations will be safeguarded;
- how local ministry will help to achieve the church's mission or grow new disciples;
- and what other more fruitful alternative shapes of ministry might be conceived.

Working together effectively

Stopping on a regular basis to consider topics such as the following ensures that the way of working matches the desired outcomes (Katzenbach and Smith in Whitney *et al.* 2004, p. 6).

- Are we clear why we're meeting? What are we trying to achieve? Are we recognizing that an interdependent culture is essential? How will we know if we achieve our object? What virtues and habits would we want this team or group to be known for?
- Does everyone know their role and responsibility, separately and together? Does each person here know what he or she has to contribute? What would help members enact to a high standard the virtues and habits of the group? What would help the group go beyond their present expectations of themselves? How can each person find the adult maturity to allow for learning through recognizing mistakes or failures?
- Is there mutual support and encouragement? How do members relate to one another so that everyone learns and grows through the tasks given to the group? How will it be clear that every person has a unique and necessary part to play? How is mutual respect and appreciation fostered as part of the group's task and ways of working?
- What will be the open and clear methods of working? What will make the procedures of meetings most inclusive so that everyone contributes to the outcome? How are decisions made so that everyone is committed to the implementation?
- How will leaders both affirm and critique? How will appointed leaders work with everyone, together and individually? How can

leadership be corporate? What will be needed for everyone to know they have a part to play in the power dynamics so they can truly make a difference? How does the leader facilitate this?

- Where does new energy emerge? If a team is to keep momentum, what virtues and habits will allow for regeneration? In what ways will positive outcomes be marked and celebrated?
- How is team performance to be monitored? What will be the connection between the team and those on whose behalf it formed? What are the ways of knowing that work is being achieved? What quality assurance methods will be needed?
- How will the team communicate? How will excellent communication, inside and outside the group, be at a premium to allow each person to participate fully? What needs to be communicated?

Effective task groups and teams return to these questions often, and always when there is a change in the membership. However, in a developing participatory church, according to the numbers involved and any clustering with others, it will be the entire body that needs to be known for its chosen virtues and necessary habits.

Local church(es) acting as 'team(s)'

Churches that are shaped in wisdom and virtues rather than regulations and repetition are essentially untidy, diverse, loosely organized and unpredictable. Although tasks can be assigned and responsibilities distributed, at any moment new circumstances can emerge: illness, unemployment, redeployment, a family crisis, bereavement or simply the need to be nurtured for a while, rather than being a source of energy. Essentially people are a 'given' in their church, which raises the important *episkope* question very practically. As well as including everyone who offers, there has to be wise discernment before people can be blessed into public acts for the community (ministry as distinct from discipleship).

In small-scale churches, of course, everyone just gets on with things together as best they can and lives with the awareness of everyone's foibles. In more complex churches the priest, wardens and church council will need to have courage, for the health of the whole community, to discern whether individuals are best fitted for roles.

The story circulates of a unusually honest church council meeting in which a prominent member offered himself to read from Scripture more frequently as 'he knew he had a special gift in that direction'. He met with a resounding, 'Oh no, you're not! You're rubbish at reading in church but you're brilliant at making people welcome, so please do some more of that!'

It takes time to get to know the interests, skills and ways of relating of others. How can this person contribute for his or her good and for the flourishing of the whole church? What would she bring from other parts of her life? How would he balance other commitments and relationships with what the church might be asking at this time? Some churches have benefited from inviting people to be interviewed or to interview one another as a way of helping them to spell out what they believe to be core practices of faith and how they can contribute.

Collaborative ministry makes more demands of priesthood. We invest hugely in careful processes of selection, demanding programmes of formation. Priests make solemn vows indicating a distinctive and *at the same time* deeply relational role for the flourishing of the Church for the world. In generosity, service and friendship the priest holds authority, intuitively practising an art and being willing to grow into the relational ontology of priesthood. And in various ways this is true of all public ministries.

This gives the priest an authority to help keep the local church true to its virtues and habits, the way it is formed and re-formed in its identity. So in my experience of leading a diverse team of lay and ordained leaders who in turn animate other leaders, my role is:

- regularly to help the team and therefore the community discern its priorities (within all the routines of designing and delivering worship and ensuring pastoral care);
- to hold everyone to these priorities or help negotiate when new demands require a change of emphasis;
- to keep everyone communicating so that the current priorities are known, planned and budgeted;
- to make time for each individual leader – or to make provision for someone else – to be supported in his or her particular contribution, to constantly make provision for succession and to help each leader to be aware of the wider picture;

- to press people hard when they are not delivering what they promised and to try to find ways of knowing why this is the case and what other support might be needed, including reducing their workload or allowing some piece of work to take a back seat for a while;
- to ensure that the work of individuals and groups is constantly reviewed;
- to teach practical theology that helps the team and the community discern their pictures of God in all this, especially when there is a temptation to overwork and neglect other important commitments in their lives as a whole;
- to be realistically aware, with all the staff team, of both the potential and the limits at any one time of the human resources available, in order to ensure the exercise of mutual pastoral care.

Is this a personal charism (virtue) that some carry naturally? Can it be taught and learnt like the craft of writing or being a parent – drawing on long-term warrior-like commitment, the development of realm of imagination, empathy, intuition, judgement, presence and discernment? We so easily fall into the habit of overworking and trying to make Church happen through our personal great caring and effort. It is part of the ordination promises to remain open for the gift still to be stirred up within us. Jesus prayed to his Father before anyone else was around.

In our circumstances, what will we do? We have to take time – and see it as a key element of our role to make space for study and being allured towards and overwhelmed by God. We are resourced in priestly presiding from Scripture, role models, theology, ordinary examples of genuine human cooperation, those who care for us, reflection on organizational process and essentially from our being present to our deepest core, the place where we have an intense encounter with God. And that will vary among different temperaments and opportunities – whether it is contemplation, study, walking, painting or whatever.

Whatever the rhetoric of collaborative ministry, our leadership is going to be extremely significant for the local church. The ethos, agenda, horizons and permissions all emanate from ourselves. So we need to support the church in working out how it will be identified as

Church, rather than as some other organization. How we encourage local churches to show Christ's love inviting a response will be in the quality of relationships and chosen practices, rather than in theories and models.

This requires priests and other leaders to make it a priority to empower people, in each local church, in an intense listening exercise. This naturally happens now whenever parish profiles are prepared or local ministry teams are spawned or renewed, so the agenda now is to embed this virtue through the everyday practices of church life. We face a dilemma, as over centuries we have relied on priests to such an extent to carry out the mission of the Church that there are now so few in the congregations who have the motivation, self-expectation or inner resource for this.

As priests we must be secure enough not to guard our traditional turf. Part of being lured by God into faith and discipleship is to know that God's kind of power has open hands. This releases us to evoke and nurture faith and leadership in many others. For this we need a vibrant working notion of Church, an ecclesiology, that excites us and that we can teach and practise in many different ways. Unless we have this sense of a relational Church serving a relational God, we shall not extricate ourselves from the habits of clericalism and the Church will not experience liberation.

Rise up in love! Christmas to Trinity through St John's Gospel

A very recent example of the kind of community freedom and focus of which I speak was an initial planning meeting to check out an idea of mine and to take soundings with a self-selecting group. After opening worship I described how I was reading the situation in the congregation. For a number of years we had explored important new aspects of worship, learning and mission. Spirit-led church life moves in waves and not straight lines: times for being energetic and times for pondering what we have learnt and remembering that God loves us for nothing. Some of the leaders needed to move more slowly for a while and a good number of people new to the church needed to be nurtured in prayer and faith.

I then suggested we allow St John's Gospel to be a vehicle on which to travel through from the following Christmas to Trinity Sunday. Through worship, study and contemplation we could build a simple programme that nurtured the congregation as walking in the way of Jesus. I briefly picked out themes in the chapters of St John's Gospel, noticing how many of them resonated with life in the Church and world today. Then I offered a possible framework of worship and learning that matched the liturgical calendar. For example, I suggested Ash Wednesday as a quiet day in church. Instead of organizing Lent groups, we could open the church several times through each week, with a small amount of structure and an inviting atmosphere for prayer, with optional conversation groups. And again on the first three days of Holy Week we could explore through the characters of the beloved disciples, Peter and Judas, our own responses to the love of Jesus. We then broke into small groups for conversation.

The main responses recorded by one of the wardens were:

- There was a consensus that it was a really good idea to focus on John's Gospel for a time of nurturing.
- It would encourage everyone to read John's Gospel and to understand it better.
- The focus could be used right the way through from Christmas to Pentecost; it should include Mothering Sunday even though at first glance this might be more difficult, but John has plenty of positive focus on women and on Jesus' relationship with his mother, for example, the wedding at Cana.
- Starting Holy Week on the Saturday, as 'the day of Lazarus', when the authorities finally decided to have Jesus arrested, was a good idea.
- Not just for Sunday mornings: how to do it so that it doesn't just become reading John on Sunday mornings? A need to make connections through the week as well.
- Points on Lent groups/Bible study/intentional conversations:
  - working in small groups allows less confident people to ask questions and discuss;
  - getting people into church and drawing in people who would do Lent groups;
  - including aspects that people get out of Lent groups;
  - linking what people get out of Lent groups with what we do;
  - arranging conversations about Bible passages;
  - including sharing food together.

- The quiet day idea was well received but there was a question about the best day.
- On opening church up in Lent, there was a commitment to making it happen for two or three hours each day. When should it be: afternoon for those who don't want to come out in evening, or evening for those occupied during the day? A rota of people could be made to provide opportunity for quiet prayer, *lectio divina* or brief teaching, as appropriate. It would be a good shared discipline to provide this. Even if only the person opening up the church was there and no one else turned up, it would have an effect on the continuity, sense of commitment and flow.
- All of this needs further thought and effective communication.

Those who put themselves into this, apart from myself as parish priest, were a mixture of men and women, ordained and lay. Some had previously experienced a year of spiritual growth in the parish that I had led five years earlier and they spoke of the confidence they had received from it and hoped that this process would have a similar outcome for many others. What I believe this narrative illustrates is the desire for growth in spirituality and in articulating and celebrating faith and drawing in others. It reminds me of the importance for priests and colleagues of not being so absorbed in managing the ministries of others that we do not feed the community from our particular skills and gifts. Occasions like this continue to give me a sense of hope for a Church when the practice of expanding opportunities for people to be drawn towards God is made a long-term priority.

13

Integrating wholeness

Being drawn by God's Spirit in the whole of life

The world stands in need of a miracle. Its regeneration cannot simply be a natural process, and in so many respects the disruptions of sin have wrought a chaos that exceeds humanity's power to put right. What Christianity proclaims, however, is that the miracle has already taken place. With the raising of Jesus from the dead, the creation has been restored to life with the Father ... That communion with the one through whom the world was made, and in whom all things hold together is the only basis upon which all things will ever be made new (Revelation 21.5).

(Murray Rae 2006, p. 211)

Holding everything together

To love God for God's sake is inseparable from loving the people and the world God loves. Yet this double involvement in God and neighbour is not done in isolation; it requires a community, a school of desire and wisdom that is concerned for both God and the world and within which people can be formed in faith, hope and love.

When the Church frustrates and hurts us, the real temptation is to leave behind all the communal, institutional, organizational mess and choose to grow deeper into God. We reject the temporal matters of buildings, disputes, finance, land, law, bishops, priests, church councils and community dynamics, and long instead for a simple, uncluttered, private spirituality. The relational understanding of God and our response in lattices of community living has been a powerful current in all that has been written here. Despite the many clashes I have known with the Church's worst habits, my hope remains for knowing God through common worship, community, sacrament, buildings, structures, communication networks, friendship and connection with many groups of Christians past and contemporary.

To summarize the tracers of this in the argument so far:

- Although clearly Jesus personally made an intense impact on individuals who were healed or unbound from sin, his ministry was largely in teams of various sizes.
- The pictures and narratives Jesus employed to show the nature of the Father's kingdom were mostly relational.
- From the earliest days after the resurrection, followers of Jesus met to pray, praise God, break bread and share possessions for the sake of those in need.
- The Eucharist, the key act of Christian worship, is a gathering of worshippers of many kinds.
- Creedal agreement comes through centuries of dispute as a collective statement is recognized as a priority.
- The continually revisited practices of the community are the ways in which Christian faith is restated and embodied in new situations.
- A binary world–spirituality view is completely inconsistent with the Trinitarian wisdom of God's being and the relational understanding of all Creation.
- Virtue ecclesiology needs the local church and the institutional Church to seek excellence in the same virtues and practices.

So despite everything that can be tragic and despair-making about the Church and its interface with society, the practice of Christian faith is inherently corporate and relational. It matters, therefore, that we check out our virtues and practices against the larger canvas of twenty centuries of Christian endeavour to find adequate speech about God and God's ways with the world.

Mistakes about God become mistakes about Church and priesthood

Building on the work of nineteenth-century Schleiermacher on four natural Christian heresies, Stephen Pickard has suggested that mistakes about a Christian understanding of God get rolled over into mistakes about Church and ministry practice. A Church with no significant Trinitarian doctrine of God will pick up imperial or military images that separate a visible from an invisible Church, will regard the Spirit as the earthly Church's possession, rather than the one to follow, and so emphasizes unity that there is no room for diversity.

When Christ's humanity is diminished, the Church and its ministry cannot recognize their own frailty and the clergy become identified as the holy ones. In reality this is unbelievable, but many churches operate (with architecture and liturgy to match) with a sense of the clergy representing Christ in glory, with the laity possibly representing Jesus of Nazareth, if they are given sufficient knowledge of him.

The Church in every age has found itself in difficulty in holding together the transcendent holiness and the down-to-earth real presence of God. Our difficulty with managing the tension between things so-called 'temporal' and 'spiritual' is partly a result of our difficulties in understanding how Jesus is like us as human beings and different from us in order to be our Redeemer. The heresy of 'docetism', in which it only seemed that Christ shared our human nature, has its opposite in the Nazarean or Ebionite heresy of regarding Jesus as just an ordinary human being. When the balance is lost towards the divinity of Christ, there is a consequent sacred inflation of the Church as a spiritual elite unconcerned with merely practical matters. When there is an overemphasis on the humanity of Christ, then the Church becomes just one social institution among others.

Pickard identifies many ways in which the Church acts out of character as a result of its theology of God being awry. Sometimes this presents as rampant individualism, lack of intimacy between persons, anxiety leading to overworking, a lack of confidence in the Spirit's guiding, an overemphasis on management theories to the detriment of the present activity of Godself or sharp boundaries drawn between the Church and the world, the sacred and the profane. A dynamic ecclesiology of the whole people of God is the basis on which this book is written. What habits and practices will best ensure confidence in churches working easily with buildings, finance, local authorities and Scripture, learning programmes, sermons, sacraments and spiritual accompaniment, for instance?

Planning formational programmes

The 2012 Common Awards process for re-imagining ministerial formation takes the Church of England, institutionally, into a holistic set of virtues and practices. There is no doubt that 'there remains only a narrow window to alter the current paradigm of both training for ministry and ministry itself' in a church and educational culture of institutional inertia (Martin 2012, p. 92). In local churches the most moving transformational learning processes draw out the whole of people and draw those of all ages together in a way that is counter-cultural. Leaders speak of learning more than they were able to give. Love for God and neighbour is intensified and appreciated when difference is seen to build a great community spirit. This awareness must be recognized as a vital clue for identifying church life and the work of the priest now.

How parishes plan the process for intergenerational learning is a vital virtue for today. It is one of the leading themes in the Church of England's Common Awards proposals. In *Being God's People* (Greenwood and Hart 2011), Sue Hart and I presented a theory–practice account of our method of drawing people closer into belief and worship. Table 13.1 overleaf is an example of the minutes of our parish learning core group to indicate the detailed practice of working with a team to make Christian learning attractive, participative and accessible. In the accompanying list I identify some of the practices that constitute this intentionally transformational and participative pedagogy in what we call 'The Magical Mystery Tour' and 'YouThink'.

Practices that make this come alive, either in a single large church or in a group of churches in collaboration, include:

- a lay leader with long experience in educational management who is actively training and coaching others to become leaders;
- a great emphasis on reflection on experience;
- accepting all that people bring;
- long-term detailed planning;
- energetic advertising and promotion;
- personal invitation;
- recognizing when there's too much on offer and waiting till another time;
- linking learning with public worship and training people to lead;

Table 13.1 Minutes of the parish learning core group

Theme: Learning, living and sharing
Vision: To lead and deliver discipleship and evangelizing strategies in accordance with our mission to all ages across the parish
Who: Sue (coordinator), Trisha, Mike, Katherine, Suzy and Craig
Date: 7 May 2012

Actions	Timescale	Planned outcome
Lent 2012	Completed	Successful Lent 2012 course with BBC's *The Passion*, with a total of 70–80+ people engaging with learning group resources. Follow up with evening worship in September (see below)
Café Church	Postponed	Postponed indefinitely through lack of take-up. Will continue to bring up at future meetings in case there becomes a more appropriate time to do this
Magical Mystery Tour (MMT) 2012	14 August 2012 – 14 July 2013	Dates and destinations already planned in principle with the first three sessions due for detailed planning 12 July 2012, when dates will be finalized. Posters ready to be put up in church to advertise further
The Passion – evening worship and future thoughts	16 September 2012	Evening worship to address final questions that arose out of Lent 2012 Passion course. To be worked up more fully and advertised in August. Craig to work on getting questions in a useable form, hoping to get through about six to eight on the night. Sue to plan the format of the evening and order of service; expected worship with group discussion

Table 13.1 (continued)

Actions	Timescale	Planned outcome
Jesus course	Autumn	Lindisfarne Regional Training Partnership course: 'Who is Jesus?' Understanding that this is a course typically run over five weeks aimed at growing Christians Is delivered by David and so won't be too involving for learning group Sue has contacted Robin about this, more information shortly
YouThink	Continuing	Plan to adapt some of the resources used in MMT 2012–13 for Suzy to use with YouThink Will revisit again once MMT is under way to think of a time-scale to get this going
Lent	Not yet decided	
Short study courses	Autumn/winter	Trisha has produced two sessions for the course Sue has adapted plan for session 1 for delivering to a group at St Mary's to discuss with Trisha First session on 'What does repentance really mean?' Expected to be aimed at those who want a deeper understanding of Christian faith issues
'Shock of the New' – baptism families		An idea to deliver a 'Shock of the New' experience to baptism families and those new to the church, very light learning, in the context of sharing food and fellowship Sue to discuss those willing to be involved with the baptism group and plan sessions again with Val

- seeing how one course connects with another and sharing resources;
- working ecumenically, but often deliberately within our own tradition, which is very broad anyway;
- noticing that, while process is a very important element in learning, sometimes a taught course is very attractive;
- finding ways of linking formation with those who bring children for baptism.

Holistic institutional Church

Church arises in places where companionship in Christ is already experienced in mutual understanding, forgiveness, transformation and reconciliation with one another and with God. The breaking of bread and sharing wine in the Eucharist is the visible and tangible practice that makes real a life of companionship. It is in the practical experience of God's hospitality in which an eschatological hope and advance sign is nurtured of the household of the Father, the Son and the Holy Spirit.

I can illustrate the argument of this chapter by exploring how in a parish church or a cluster of churches the temporalities and spiritualities are held together in the everyday work of a vicar and colleagues, lay or ordained. The vicar in a complex network of churches may hopefully collaborate effectively with a team and therefore is not expected to be omnicompetent. But she or he cannot be unaware of or choose to have no knowledge of any significant element in the whole running of the operation.

So, for example, at any one time some of the following aspects of *the church*'s life will be demanding attention and skill: drafting of discussing a liturgy for a forthcoming event, being involved in some aspect of music, negotiating with other parishes and clergy locally, preparing adult learning or sermons, meeting with other leaders of pieces of work, relating to the local schools, seeking funding for a new project, taking care in discerning who might fulfil a new role and give up one occupied for a while, discussing architect's plans, caring pastorally for someone in the congregation and neighbourhood, and taking a part in local or civic life.

Holding this together with caring for oneself and family and taking time for study and work consultancy makes for a demanding and complex role. The point here is that there is nothing that is of no interest to the vicar, even if many of these issues are someone else's primary task, and there can be no authentic polarization. In other words, it won't do for the vicar to have no interest in the accounts or the music or the liturgy because together their practice builds up virtues towards the final purpose of the church(es) for the sake of the kingdom, however that may be expressed in context.

So in discerning how to be Church, Christian communities and clergy are not free to separate out spirituality and bricks and mortar or kindness and management or freedom and leadership. The Spirit speaks to the whole community in all its life, welfare and mission planning. In the Acts of the Apostles there is no doubt that the Spirit touches individuals personally and deeply, such as Paul, Peter and Stephen. But although they were conscious of the inner movement of the Spirit, they were sent and received by communities, they discerned together as a group that the Spirit did not want them to preach in Bithynia or Asia Minor but was calling them to Macedonia. The whole community was listening and responding to the voice of the Spirit.

The work of priest and churches now is to be sufficiently open to the Spirit to discern what communal practices will best serve God's desire for the wholeness of the world and its people. This assumes that churches take time to become communities who love one another in Christ, pray together and listen and watch for where the Spirit is already at work, both among them and in the neighbourhood. Such a church will be aware of the particular gifts given to each of its members. Communal discernment is a vital element in becoming Church now.

What society needs now are church communities that create gospel-shaped structures rooted in virtues and habits that can go on being lived in, reflected on and revised. Those formed in a world governed by duty, conformity, obedience to authority and intermittent contact with a transcendent God of uniformity must recognize that, for Church to serve new generations, they have to risk allowing others to participate. We may disapprove, but choice, not obedience, is the key for younger people now. It's no longer satisfying for the expert to tell us the meaning of the Bible or the history of the saints. The expert cannot be patient and wait ten years before he or she can be on the church council.

A self-organizing, mutually ordered community that echoes Trinitarian relating in the Spirit will always be moving in response to circumstances and the arrival of new people. Café-style meetings and worship are often used today. Essentially this is about empowering the voice of everyone present through listening to one another, exchanging views on urgent topics, formulating responses, summarizing and designing ways forward to which most people can assent. It is a notable example of a practice which, if prepared and led with care, is a potent agent for developing confidence and mutual respect in church and community (see <www.theworldcafe.com>). The processes of world café and Appreciative Inquiry allow for genuine complexity as churches wrestle with authority patterns, and increasingly in multiple benefices and varying contexts. The task now is for local churches to find identity without being at war with other churches, or even among the membership. Living with and celebrating difference and questions within a stable and ordered community is what many seek and would be willing to contribute to wholeheartedly. How can this be when leadership has been reserved to clergy for so long and when now those clergy are increasingly stretched beyond measure?

Increasingly, stipendiary priests are expected to be competent and even to flourish in overseeing a cluster of parishes, each with a different take on God and on how they see the world. If we refer back to Torbert's action-logics (page 41), it's clear that much more help is required to match priest to tasks in the first place, but that then mentoring is required to encourage moving on from being experts, working out of what has been learnt at college. One of the benefits of taking the action-logic perspective – almost out of focus, rather than literally – is that it allows us to review ourselves and see how we have moved. 'That's how I used to be limited but now I can see more; and further, I really want to become an "alchemist".' The reality is that, at different moments, we're all of those logics. The alchemist seems an attractive image to me because it's a figure who is unpredictable, both available and remote, attached and also detached, and so able to offer the community a variety of interventions and gifts.

For this movement to take place we need support in letting go of control and benign domination, so we can draw others into participation and sharing a larger perspective. Many of the *laos* know this in their family and work. It takes a confident diocese, parish and priest to invite them to live to the full within the Church, especially when this makes things uncomfortable. It is a particularly difficult time for churches, and the intensive engagement with God in all the ways we have explored is the route we must take.

Holding together the theoretical with the practical, the spiritual with the institution, dioceses and churches must take more time to grow the complex and agile workforce that they need while maintaining and improving the everyday performance of Church for the health of society. Priests, leaders and teams have a responsibility to make time, crucially, to transform themselves and the networks for which they are responsible. In a wildly diverse and loosely affiliated Church, helping everyone to build the capacity to thrive in a complex world is a priority now.

Communities and priests formed in Trinitarian wisdom

Throughout this study has been a realistic awareness of just how demanding it is in the present time, emotionally and physically, to be a Christian community and an ordained animator of churches. I have searched for sources of encouragement in Scripture, in theology and in organizational theory and practice. Vitally, becoming who we are as persons, most fully through stepping into God's own relational livingness, has been interwoven in this study with becoming Church again in new circumstances. I have given instances of where Church is emerging within a relational and hospitable understanding of God and life. The proposal of linking the wisdom tradition with possibilities for a virtue ecclesiology suggests a walking ecclesiology focused on Jesus Christ as the ultimate place of contact and communication between God and humanity through seeking excellence in detailed practices. In the spirit of Rahner's nameless virtue and of the interpersonal nature of the Trinity, I have attempted a flowing movement between practice and theory so that the being of Church and priesthood is also the act. *Who we are is what we do.*

In the particular work of priesthood I have purposely insisted that it can only be imagined, spoken of and practised within a total, holistic vision of Church. Priesthood has the incarnational dimension of being rooted and ordered in particular places and times. It also has the eschatological dimension of discerning God's deepest desire for persons, churches and neighbourhoods and imagining and walking with them towards their truest potential. Priests therefore have a particular responsibility to grow in self-awareness and to build that capacity into the communities among which they live and where they help identify the character of communities, especially by animating their Eucharistic celebrations.

The ordering together of all the baptized in the spirit of mutual love and in profound difference has to be embodied especially among those who are ordained or licensed to demonstrate that whole shared *episkope* aspect of Church in which all are called to participate. Despite the Church's brokenness and blindness, Christian wisdom is that love is constituted ecclesially in worship and in the eschatological work of drawing together in Christ the whole world in the power of the Spirit to serve the Father's desire.

Some of the most significant moments at conferences often come unexpectedly in chance conversation. Recently at a national consultation, over lunch someone said to me, 'I agree with what you are saying, but what do I do if the people don't want it?' By this he meant, 'It's so tough where I am because I find such a negative attitude towards a Church that is mutual and relational, preferring to be passive and part of a linear hierarchy.' In human terms, becoming Church again is simply exhausting.

Moments like that make me think fast and hard and we discussed the responsibility of the presiding priest to hold local churches to catholic ordering within the world Church. I think many clergy and laity find themselves in such a tough place, and from my experience the following are a raft of ways in which the texture of local churches can evolve towards a communion rather than hierarchical way of being:

- Talk openly about God as Trinity so that initial embarrassment gives way to others feeling comfortable to do the same; let prayers include both fixed forms and words perhaps written on Post-it® notes or agreed in a conversation first.
- Promote a variety of ways in which we gather for worship, prayer and meetings: be subversive in practically arranging the furniture to allow for face-to-face engagement, expecting dialogue, reducing chances for dependency; make such spaces before anyone arrives or encourage first arrivals to see the point and join in; keep moving the furniture to suit the purpose of the gathering; be resilient even

if this means using screwdrivers or saws: there is too much at stake to be looking over our shoulders at those who fixed the seating years ago.

- Conduct worship and meetings with serious intent and yet with humanity and humour: ordered spontaneity ensures the task is achieved but not without building the community and encouraging individuals.
- Include refreshments, however simple; light a gathering candle; make a hospitable space with rocks, icons, pieces of coloured material or whatever comes to hand; encourage movement between the larger group, smaller groups and talking in pairs.
- Experiment, say at Advent, with services of the word in the darkness that may initially be written by clergy or Readers but are planned and presented by an intergenerational team; try out lots of different forms of worship; keep reflecting with people on the learning that is taking place.
- Work hard on inclusive language without gimmicks; try various Scripture translations and paraphrases.
- Include young ones by early preparation for Holy Communion; invite a range of visitors from the wider Church who will cheerfully reinforce all these inclusive messages about the tone and texture of Church.
- Encourage team-working; free up people who have held tasks for too long; tease people into being more relaxed and direct; allow safe space for vigorous debate and exchange of different views; find new skills for conflict management; draw in younger people to leadership roles, appreciate and support them and expect older people to do the same.
- Keep teaching in different styles that the gospel is inherently relational and so much the genuine and attractive practice of Church.
- Design the liturgy to reinforce participation and to subvert hierarchy without denying that at different moments the presider, the lay reader, the intercessor and the singers take a lead – as in a jazz band.
- Ensure that when the eucharistic bread and wine is 'shared' (not 'administered'), the sick receive first, then the musicians, the laity, the eucharistic ministers and finally the presider.

This quiet evolution is vital and possible. It will depend on the vision and determination of the leadership team as well as the gradual reception of the message by a critical mass of people. Essentially, intense encounter with God through worship, Scripture, silence and many forms of prayer is the only way. In the accounts of Jesus' ministry of healing, forgiving and restoring to common life, it is God's life in him that allows for the saving work to take place. While priests and churches offer as external goods (in MacIntyre's terms) language about God, practices of public worship, of being forgiven and restored and of justice can only be authentic and transformational if there are matching internal goods.

To break down the false self (co-created by so many influences) that inhibits churches and priests from being real and truthful demands that we allow the Holy Spirit to inhabit, open, inform and lead us. It is the Holy Spirit that Jesus promises to send to the disciples after the resurrection so that the Church 'will do greater works than these' (John 14.12).

After more than seven years as parish priest with a large team in a suburban parish, I'm relieved to know that God takes the long-term view and is Lord of all, far more than the single span of one incumbency. Also with *episkope* as a key characteristic of Church, it is in the interwoven ministries of many, over time, that God's purposes are achieved. The laity know from their own experience in institutions and work places that it's hard to sustain energy and innovation over a number of years when there are so many other draws on one's time. Part of the task of a parish priest is to prepare people for our leaving. If we abandon linear progress through hard work and live in God's grace, I think it's possible to let go of 'success' and consider instead long-term sustainability and the belief that over a given period some lives will have been deeply touched by God.

As priests and people, we are pilgrims, ordered together and ordered specifically. Our common task is to make known what we have seen of the Risen Christ and to follow practices that contribute to the world's consummation. The same Spirit who filled Jesus, Paul and John is here when we assemble to pray, attend to Scripture, discern and celebrate the Eucharist. The Holy Spirit is the one in whom we can have hope of becoming Church, through practices of mutual love, respect and reconciliation. Maria Boulding reflecting on reading Augustine, writes:

In the whole Christ, Head and members together, the new creation is carried forward, like an unstoppable explosion from the radiant centre ... Christian mysticism is being taken up into the mystery, the mystery that is Christ; it is to allow the whole of our lives to be drawn into the light of his cross and resurrection (Ephesians 1.18).   (Boulding 2010, pp. 135f.)

Jesus, after his baptism, is pushed out into the wilderness by the Spirit to discover at the deepest level the shape of God's call and his identity. It was only then that, filled with the power of the Holy Spirit, Jesus could return to Galilee (Luke 4.14). Are we ready to accept the Spirit's invitation to the desert in the same frame of mind as Jesus' desiring to be the most faithful witness to God's desire, however painful the cost? Dare we open ourselves again to the Holy Spirit and the uncompromising vocation of the risen life of God's people? For this we have no alternative but to lose ourselves in worship of the Trinitarian God in company with reckless and hopeful saints, prophets and martyrs who show us there is no other way.

References and suggestions
for further reading

Avis, Paul (2000) 'Ministry', in Adrian Hastings *et al.* (eds) *The Oxford Dictionary of Christian Thought*, Oxford University Press, Oxford, p. 437.

Barker, Pat (1991) *Regeneration*, Viking, London.

Boulding, Maria, OSB (2010) *Gateway to Resurrection*, Continuum, London.

Bowes, Peter Hugh (2012) 'Future Church: envisioning the Church of England in Southern Ryedale in the second decade of the 21st century', doctoral thesis, Durham University. Available at Durham E-Theses Online: <http://etheses.dur.ac.uk/3509/>.

Brown, David (2006) *Releasing Bishops for Relationships*, Foundation for Church Leadership, London.

Brown, Juanita and Isaacs, David (2005) *The World Café: Shaping our futures through conversations that matter*, Berrett–Koehler, San Francisco.

Buxton, Alyson (2012) 'Rural ministry: a brief overview and reflection', unpublished essay.

Buxton, Graham (2001) *Dancing in the Dark: The privilege of participating in the ministry of Christ*, Paternoster Press, Carlisle.

Chittister, Joan (2008) *The Gift of Years*, Darton, Longman and Todd, London.

Church of England (2011) *General Synod: Formation for Ministry and framework for Higher Education Validation: Phase 2 Report of the Working Party, as approved by the House of Bishops, December 2011*, available at: <http://churchofengland.org/media/1386203/gs%20misc%201008%20-%20higher%20education%20frunding%20changes%20%28phase%202%29.pdf >.

Clinton, Michael (2011) *Experiences of Ministry Survey*, Church of England and King's College London, London.

Clore, Gerald L. (2012) 'Psychology and the rationality of emotion', in Sarah Coakley (ed.) *Faith, Rationality and the Passions*, Wiley-Blackwell, Oxford.

Coakley, Sarah (2012) 'God and gender: how theology can find a way through the impasse', *ABC Religion and Ethics*, 8 March, p. 3; available at: <www.abc.net.au/religion/articles/2012/03/08/>.

Coelho, Paulo (1999) *The Alchemist*, HarperCollins, London.

Collins, John N. (1990) *Diakonia: Reinterpreting the Ancient Sources*, Oxford University Press, New York.

Collins, John N. (1992) *Are All Christian Ministers?* Liturgical Press, Collegeville, MN.

Cray, Graham, Mobsby, Ian and Kennedy, Aaron (eds) (2010) *New Monasticism as Fresh Expression of Church*, Canterbury Press, Norwich.

Diemer, Paul (1990) *Love without Measure: Extracts from the writings of Bernard of Clairvaux*, Darton, Longman and Todd, London.

Dollard, Kit, Marett-Crosby, Anthony, OSB, and Wright, Timothy, OSB (2002) *Doing Business with Benedict: The Rule of Saint Benedict and business management: a conversation*, Continuum, London.

Everist, Norma Cook (ed.) (2002) *The Difficult but Indispensable Church*, Fortress Press, Minneapolis.

Feldman, Christina (2005) *Compassion: Listening to the cries of the world*, Rodmell Press, Berkeley, California.

Finley, James, Rohr, Richard and Bourgeault, Cynthia (2012) *Following the Mystics through the Narrow Gate* (available as CD, DVD or download for MP3), Rohr Institute, Albuquerque, New Mexico.

Ford, David F. (1999) *Self and Salvation: Being transformed*, Cambridge University Press, Cambridge.

Ford, David F. (2007) *Christian Wisdom: Desiring God and learning in love*, Cambridge University Press, Cambridge.

Forder, C. (1947) *The Parish Priest at Work*, SPCK, London.

Freire, P. (2000, 30th anniversary edition) *Pedagogy of the Oppressed*, Continuum, London.

Gebara, Ivone (1999) *Longing for Running Water*, Fortress Press, Minneapolis.

Gray-Reeves, Mary, and Perham, Michael (2011) *The Hospitality of God: Emerging worship for a missional church*, Seabury Books, New York.

Greenwood, Robin (1996) *Practising Community: The task of the local church*, SPCK, London.

Greenwood, Robin (2000) *The Ministry Team Handbook: Local ministry as partnership*, SPCK, London,

Greenwood, Robin (2002) *Transforming Church: Liberating structures for ministry*, SPCK, London.

Greenwood, Robin (2009) *Parish Priests: For the sake of the kingdom*, SPCK, London.

Greenwood, Robin and Burgess, Hugh (2005) *Power*, SPCK, London.

Greenwood, Robin and Hart, Sue (2011) *Being God's People: The confirmation and discipleship handbook*, SPCK, London.

Greenwood, Robin and Pascoe, Caroline (2006) *Local Ministry: Story, process and meaning*, SPCK, London.

Grundy, Malcolm (2011) *Leadership and Oversight. New models for episcopal ministry*, Mowbray, London.

Guardian (2012) Obituary of Tony Marsh, 23 April.

Guite, Malcolm (2012) *Faith, Hope and Poetry*, Ashgate, London.

Hardy, Daniel W. (2001) *Finding the Church*, SCM, London.

Hardy, Daniel W. (2010) *Wording a Radiance: Parting conversations on God and the Church*, SCM, London.

Heywood, David (2011) *Reimagining Ministry*, SCM, London.

Honoré, Carl (2004) *In Praise of Slowness: How a worldwide movement is challenging the cult of speed*, HarperCollins, San Francisco.

Janzen, David (2005) 'Intentional formation in the way of Christ and the rule of the community along the lines of the old novitiate', in the Rutba House (ed.) *School(s) for Conversion: 12 marks of a New Monasticism*, Cascade Books, Eugene, OR.

Johnson, Elizabeth A. (1998) *She Who Is. The mystery of God in feminist discourse*, Crossroad Herder, New York.

Johnston, William (1999) *Being in Love: A practical guide to Christian prayer*, Fordham University Press, New York.

Katzenbach, J. R. and Smith, D. K. (1993) *The Wisdom of Teams*, HarperCollins, New York.

Kearney, Richard (2006) *Navigations: Collected Irish essays 1976–2006*, Syracuse University Press, Syracuse, New York.

LaCugna, Catherine Mowry (1991) *God for Us: The Trinity and Christian life*, HarperCollins, San Francisco.

Lartey, Emmanuel Y. (2006) *Pastoral Theology in an Intercultural World*, Epworth Press, Peterborough.

Leech, K. (1977) *Soul Friend: A study of spirituality*, Sheldon Press, London.

Lewis, Sarah, Passmore, Jonathan and Cantore, Stefan (2011) *Appreciative Inquiry for Change Management: Using AI to facilitate organizational development*, Kogan Page, London.

Lodge, David (2011) *How Far Can You Go?*, Vintage, London (first published 1980, Secker & Warburg, London).

Lutz, Christopher Stephen (2012) *Reading Alasdair MacIntyre's After Virtue*, Continuum, London and New York.

Macfarlane, Robert (2012) *The Old Ways: A journey on foot*, Hamish Hamilton, London.

MacIntyre, A. (2007, third edition) *After Virtue*, Duckworth, London.

Mannion, Gerard (2007) *Ecclesiology and Postmodernity: Questions for the Church in our time*, The Liturgical Press, Collegeville, MN.

Martin, Simon (2012) 'Review of David Heywood's *Reimagining Ministry* (SCM, London, 2011)', *Journal of the Rural Theology Association*, 10(1): 91–2.

Merton, Thomas (2003, third edition) *New Seeds of Contemplation*, Shambhala Press, Boston, MA (first edition 1961).

Moore, Geoff (2011) 'Churches as organizations: towards a virtue ecclesiology for today', *International Journal for the Study of the Christian Church*, 11(1): 45–65.

Moore, Geoff (2012) 'The Christian Church as organization: an empirical exploration of MacIntyre's conceptual framework', working paper.

Murray, Paul (ed.) (2008) *Receptive Ecumenism and the Call to Catholic Learning: Exploring a way for contemporary ecumenism*, Oxford University Press, Oxford.

O'Brien, Bill (n.d.) 'Global Dialog Project', available at: <http://global.mit.edu/projects/project/global-dialog-project/>.

Oldham, James, Key, Tony and Starak, Yaro (1988) *Risking Being Alive*, PIT Publishing, Bundoora, Victoria, Australia.

Oliver, Mary (2010) *Wild Geese: Selected poems*, Bloodaxe Books, Tarset, Northumberland.

Oxford Centre for Ecclesiology and Practical Theology (2011) *Sustaining Leaders for Mission and Change: The continuing ministerial development of archdeacons in the Church of England*, Oxford Centre for Ecclesiology and Practical Theology, Oxford/Ripon College, Cuddesdon.

Pearson, B. (2012) 'Lone rangers – how is it for you?' available at: <www.bathandwells.org.uk/static/connect/february2011/page1.htm#story2>.

Pennington, M. Basil (2000) *True Self, False Self: Unmasking the spirit within*, Crossroad Press, New York.

Peterson, Eugene (2011) *Practise Resurrection: A conversation of growing up in Christ*, Hodder & Stoughton, London.

Pickard, Stephen (2009) *Theological Foundations for Collaborative Ministry: One of another*, Ashgate Press, Farnham.

Pickard, Stephen (2011) *In-Between God: Theology, community and discipleship*, ATF, Hindmarsh, South Africa.

Rae, Murray (2006) 'Humanity in God's world' in Alan J. Torrance and Michael Manner (eds) *The Doctrine of God and Theological Ethics*, T. & T. Clark/Continuum, London.

Rahner, Karl (1992) 'Plea for a nameless virtue', Chapter 3 of Karl Rahner, *Theological Investigations* 23, Darton, Longman and Todd, London.

Rendle, Gil (2011) *Leading Change in the Congregation: Spiritual and organizational tools for leaders*, The Alban Institute, Bethesda, Maryland.

Rendle, Gil and Mann, Alice (2003) *Holy Conversations: Strategic planning as a spiritual exercise for congregations*, The Alban Institute, Bethesda, Maryland.

Rohr, Richard (2012) 'Contemplative prayer', in *Richard's Daily Meditations*, available at: < http://myemail.constantcontact.com/Daily-Meditation--Contemplative-Prayer----September-12--2012.html?soid=1103098668616&aid=0xSRjuJ-zsg>.

Russell, A. (1980) *The Clerical Profession*, SPCK, London.

Rutba House, The (ed.) (2005) *School(s) for Conversion: 12 marks of a New Monasticism*, Cascade Books, Eugene, OR.

Sadgrove, Michael (2008) *Wisdom and Ministry: The call to leadership*, SPCK, London.

Savage, Sara and Boyd-MacMillan, Eolene (2007) *The Human Face of Church: A social psychology and pastoral theology resource for pioneer and traditional ministry*, SCM Press, London.

Scharmer, C. Otto (2009) *Theory U: Leading from the future as it emerges: The social technology of presencing*, Berrett-Koehler, San Francisco.

Sedmak, Clemens (2002) *Doing Local Theology: A guide for artisans of a new humanity*, Orbis, New York.

Streaty Wimberly, Anne E. and Parker, Evelyn L. (eds) (2002) *In Search of Wisdom: Faith formation in the Black Church*, Abingdon Press, Nashville, Tennessee.

Stump, Eleonore (2012) in Sarah Coakley (ed.) *Faith, Rationality and the Passions*, Wiley-Blackwell, Oxford.

Thew Forrester, Kevin L. (2003) *I Have Called You Friends*, Church Publishing, New York.

Thompson, Helen (1982) *Journey Towards Wholeness. A Jungian model of adult spiritual growth*, Paulist Press, Ramsey, NJ.

Tomlin, Graham (2011) *The Prodigal Spirit: The Trinity, the Church and the future of the world*, SPTC Books, London.

Torbert, Bill and associates (2004) *Action Inquiry: The secret of timely and transforming leadership*, Berrett-Koehler, San Francisco.

Vanier, Jean (2004) *Drawn into the Mystery of Jesus through the Gospel of John*, Darton, Longman and Todd, London.

Vidal, John (2012) 'Sea ice in the Arctic melts to lowest level ever recorded', *Guardian*, 15 September.

Vondey, Wolfgang (2008) *People of Bread: Rediscovering ecclesiology*, Paulist Press, Mahwah, NJ.

Wells, Samuel (2006) *God's Companions: Reimagining Christian ethics*, Blackwell, Oxford.

Wells, Samuel (2011) *What Anglicans Believe: An introduction*, Canterbury Press, Norwich.

Wells, Samuel and Coakley, Sarah (eds) (2008) *Praying for England: Priestly presence in contemporary culture*, Continuum, London.

Wheatley, Margaret J. (1999) *Leadership and the New Science: Discovering order in a chaotic world*, Berrett-Koehler, San Francisco.

Wheatley, Margaret J. (2012) *So Far From Home. Lost and found in our brave new world*, Berrett-Koehler, San Francisco.

Wheatley, Margaret and Frieze, Deborah (2011) *Walk Out Walk On: A learning journey into communities daring to live the future now*, Berrett-Koehler, San Francisco.

Whitney, Diana and Trosten-Bloom, Amanda (2003) *The Power of Appreciative Inquiry: A practical guide to positive change*, Berrett-Koehler, San Francisco.

Whitney, Diana, Trosten-Bloom, Amanda, and others (2004) *Appreciative Team Building: Positive questions to bring out the best of your team*, Universe, New York.

Wilber, Ken, Patten, Terry, Leonard, Adam and Morelli, Marco (2008) *Integral Life Practice: A 21ˢᵗ century blueprint for physical health, emotional balance, mental clarity, and spiritual awakening*, Integral Books, Boston and London.

William Temple Foundation (2008) *Glendale Alive*, William Temple Foundation, Manchester; available at: <www.williamtemplefoundation.org. uk/documents/Rural_Mission_and_Ministry_Initiative_Consultancy_ Report_100308.pdf >.

Winnicott, D. W. (1960) 'Ego distortion in terms of true and false self', in D. W. Winnicott, *The Maturational Process and the Facilitating Environment: Studies in the theory of emotional development*, International University Press, New York, pp. 140–52.

Yaconelli, Mark (2006) *Contemplative Youth Ministry: Practising the presence of Jesus with young people*, SPCK, London.